How to Write Successful Letters of Recommendation

10 Easy Steps for Reference Letters
that Your Employees, Colleagues,
Students & Friends Will Appreciate

– with Companion CD-ROM

Kimberly Sarmiento, Certified Professional Resume Writer

HOW TO WRITE SUCCESSFUL LETTERS OF RECOMMENDATION: 10 EASY STEPS FOR REFERENCE LETTERS THAT YOUR EMPLOYEES, COLLEAGUES, STUDENTS & FRIENDS WILL APPRECIATE — WITH COMPANION CD-ROM

Copyright © 2014 Atlantic Publishing Group, Inc.
1405 SW 6th Avenue • Ocala, Florida 34471 • Phone 800-814-1132 • Fax 352-622-1875
Website: www.atlantic-pub.com • E-mail: sales@atlantic-pub.com
SAN Number: 268-1250

Library of Congress Cataloging-in-Publication Data

Sarmiento, Kimberly, 1975-
  How to write successful letters of recommendation : 10 easy steps for reference letters that your employees, colleagues, students & friends will appreciate ; with companion CD-ROM / by Kimberly Sarmiento.
    pages cm
  Includes bibliographical references and index.
  ISBN 978-1-60138-612-0 (alk. paper) -- ISBN 1-60138-612-5 1. Employment references. 2. Letter writing. 3. Business writing. I. Title.
  HF5549.5.R45S27 2014
  808.06′665--dc23
                        2014037362

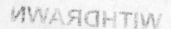

A few years back we lost our beloved pet dog Bear, who was not only our best and dearest friend but also the "Vice President of Sunshine" here at Atlantic Publishing. He did not receive a salary but worked tirelessly 24 hours a day to please his parents.

Bear was a rescue dog who turned around and showered myself, my wife, Sherri, his grandparents Jean, Bob, and Nancy, and every person and animal he met (well, maybe not rabbits) with friendship and love. He made a lot of people smile every day.

We wanted you to know a portion of the profits of this book will be donated in Bear's memory to local animal shelters, parks, conservation organizations, and other individuals and nonprofit organizations in need of assistance.

– Douglas & Sherri Brown

PS: We have since adopted two more rescue dogs: first Scout, and the following year, Ginger. They were both mixed golden retrievers who needed a home.

Want to help animals and the world? Here are a dozen easy suggestions you and your family can implement today:

- *Adopt and rescue a pet from a local shelter.*
- *Support local and no-kill animal shelters.*
- *Plant a tree to honor someone you love.*
- *Be a developer — put up some birdhouses.*
- *Buy live, potted Christmas trees and replant them.*
- *Make sure you spend time with your animals each day.*
- *Save natural resources by recycling and buying recycled products.*
- *Drink tap water, or filter your own water at home.*
- *Whenever possible, limit your use of or do not use pesticides.*
- *If you eat seafood, make sustainable choices.*
- *Support your local farmers market.*
- *Get outside. Visit a park, volunteer, walk your dog, or ride your bike.*

Five years ago, Atlantic Publishing signed the Green Press Initiative. These guidelines promote environmentally friendly practices, such as using recycled stock and vegetable-based inks, avoiding waste, choosing energy-efficient resources, and promoting a no-pulping policy. We now use 100-percent recycled stock on all our books. The results: in one year, switching to post-consumer recycled stock saved 24 mature trees, 5,000 gallons of water, the equivalent of the total energy used for one home in a year, and the equivalent of the greenhouse gases from one car driven for a year.

Dedication

*For my grandmother Carol and mother Joan, who raised,
inspired, and showed me that age really is just a number...
and for my children, Ayla & Julian, who make me feel
old and young all at the same time.*

Table of Contents

Chapter 5: Writing a Strong Letter Part Two: Content Strategy

PART THREE   145

Introduction

At every stage of academic and professional pursuits, a candidate must produce a list of references and letters of recommendation. Having earned a bachelor's and master's degree at the University of Florida, moved between states as a military wife, and restarted my career after being a stay-at-home mother, I can think of at least a dozen times when I have needed to produce letters of recommendations from very different sources.

Even now as a certified professional resume writer and business writer/content contributor, endorsements and testimonials regarding my work are essential to my web presence and business relationships. I have been in the position of asking former professors, managers, and co-workers to provide letters of recommendation (I believe I even used the couple I babysat for in high school when I was very young!) or serve as references.

Having instructed at two universities and worked in diverse business settings, I have also been called upon to write several letters of recommendations (or endorsements/testimonials) for people at varying points in their careers. Fortunately for me, writing is what I do for a living, so putting together a recommendation was not as great a challenge as I believe it is for most people.

> There are two things you must understand about letters of recommendation, such as:
>
> 1. They matter, and
> 2. You should not write a recommendation letter if you can't write a great one.

In my work as a resume writer, I have counseled many clients on how to request letters of recommendations and even found that many people's references would rather have them write the letter themselves and just sign off on it. This places a person in a conundrum, trying to figure out what to say about themselves that could sound like it came from the person they want to sign off on the letter. This is not a sound approach for the recommender or the subject of the letter.

Having maintained a solid network of associates from my graduate school days at the University of Florida, I am connected with professors at several universities across the country. I have witnessed their frustration at having students from a 300-person course ask them for a letter of recommendation. I have also witnessed the stress that letters of recommendation cause students as they wait for them to be completed and mailed as part of an application process.

I cannot emphasize enough how important the letter of recommendation is to both professional and academic candidates. It is not something that should be shrugged off or taken lightly. A letter of recommendation is not a simple reference letter. When a candidate asks for one, they are asking the writer not for an introduction, but for an evaluation of their work and qualifications for the position or school to which they are applying.

If you have never served on an admissions or selection committee or been a hiring manager, you might not realize the importance of this letter. A poorly written or weak letter can severely hurt a candidate's chances for receiving an internship or job. In the highly competitive market, this can mean the difference between an acceptance and a rejection.

There are two things you must understand about letters of recommendation, such as:

1. **They** matter, and
2. **You should not write a recommendation letter if you can't write a great one.**

"Fine," you say, *"I'm a terrible writer, so I will just decline any request that is made of me."* This is ill-advised. As I mentioned before, I have faced dozens of times when I needed letters of recommendations and testimonials for my chosen career path. If I never wrote a letter for someone else, how would my professional karma balance out?

"But you are a writer," you might say. Yes, but we are all communicators, and you can write a letter of recommendation with practice—it's just a simple letter. No matter if you excel or not in writing, you have the ability to write an astounding letter of recommendation now and then. In the technology-driven world we live in, you may have forgotten how to write a letter, but if you can easily type up an email, then you can produce a strong, impactful letter of recommendation. This book is here to help you write the best letter recommendation for a student, peer, or co-worker.

Having a basic knowledge of the person who asked you for the letter and his or her abilities and talents is a great start for creating a recommendation letter. If you can put your name on the endorsement, then this book will get you through the rest.

A 10-Step Summary

Because the name of this book begins with "10 Easy Steps", here is a basic checklist for writing letters of recommendation. These steps will be explained more in depth throughout the rest of the book. Beginning with a 'yes' or 'no' answer and ending with a follow-through, the list below tells you everything you need to write a great letter of recommendation.

1. Decide whether you should accept or reject the request to write the letter.

2. Identify the letter's requirements and your audience.

3. Review what you know about the candidate.

4. Correctly include contact information for the letter recipient and mail it on-time, if required.

5. Identify the candidate's strengths and ask if there is anything he or she wants you to highlight.

6. Include your contact information in a letterhead.

7. Write the first draft of your letter.

8. Edit your letter for grammar, brevity, content, and presentation.

9. Submit the letter via email, mail, or uploaded to a special website.

10. Be available for a follow-up.

Obviously, some of the elements on this checklist are more easily accomplished than others. In the chapters ahead, I will make recommendations and provide strategies to include everything on this list in a wide-array of situations.

Book Organization

This book is separated into three main sections. The first part defines the components of a letter of recommendation, examines whether or not you should agree to write the letter, and tells you what you need to know about the letter before you begin writing. The section also provides strong recommendations on letter writing structure, format, diction, and grammar.

The second section discusses the professional and academic letter of recommendation in detail, as well as the ways letters can differ based on the relationship between the writer and recipient. Additionally, this section reviews writing performance evaluations and networking introductions.

The third section provides sample letters of recommendations, including those for several different professions and academic pursuits. A chapter with several quick guides for letter writing is also included.

PART ONE

To write a great letter of recommendation, you need to know what makes it great or terrible. You will likely need to ask for one at some point in your career, if you already haven't. If you've never sat down to write a recommendation letter, you might not realize what needs to be included or how important they are.

The first section (the first five chapters) of this book defines what a letter of recommendation is and breaks it down into the different scenarios. This section also addresses several steps of the checklist presented in the book's introduction:

- Deciding if you should accept or reject the request to write the letter
- Identifying the letter's requirements and your audience
- Including contact information
- Writing the first draft (format, wording, grammar)
- Editing the letter for grammar and content

Letters of Recommendation Overview

Some readers may have never written a letter of recommendation before and are probably not sure why they were asked. You might not even think you are qualified to write one. Letters of recommendation are supposed to be diverse because people who know you in different capacities have unique things to say about your abilities.

For example, a student looking for admissions into college would probably ask a teacher or manager at their part-time work for a letter of recommendation. But he/she should also consider asking a youth pastor, a leader of a volunteer organization, or even a parent whose children he/she babysat. These people can talk about his or her personal qualities apart from academia, which can be very important to admissions boards.

When it comes to employment situations, a manager can use a recommendation from a team member just as much as the reverse. Nothing speaks more to your leadership abilities than being complimented by those who work for you.

Since anyone can write a letter of recommendation and speak well on behalf of a candidate, you can be confident in the knowledge that you are qualified to write the letter if you know the candidate considerably well. Now you have to overcome your inexperience of writing a letter of recommendation, or more specifically, how to write a great one.

Making sure the letter of recommendation is well written is vitally important for both the candidate and you. Writing a great letter of recommendation should help you with your networking "karma" – and networking may just be the most important skill you need to master for any job search. Simply put, the person you help get a job today could be the person who finds your next job tomorrow. In relation to the topic at hand, the person you recommend today could be a great recommender tomorrow.

Building a strong professional network takes more effort than just adding people to your LinkedIn connections. It requires that you maintain contact with individuals you do not see every day and that you respond when they reach out to you. If called upon to help or even recommend someone, endorse them as well as you can, and they will likely return the favor.

This book reviews three situations that require a letter of recommendation and multiple subsets within those situations. You will begin with the professional letter, master the academic letter, and finally learn about the networking letter. Each is important and requires a different approach to content and style, but let's start with the letter of recommendation's true definition.

Letter of Recommendation Defined

A letter of introduction was an important part of society during the 18th and 19th centuries. A person would send a letter of introduction on someone's behalf as a candidate for an apprenticeship or simply to introduce him or her into a different part of society. You can see this method of introduction demonstrated in movies and TV shows.

This custom appeared during a time when people built up their reputations like companies build up their statuses. This proved instrumental in ensuring that the beneficiary of the letter was accepted into the desired school, apprenticeship, or group if the person sending the letter of introduction had a great reputation and wrote exceptionally well. The custom allowed a person who had not yet built his/her reputation to gain leverage from an established individual. However, the letter had to be written with caution because the person you recommended could negatively impact your reputation if he/she behaved poorly after you vouched for him/her.

While society has changed significantly, the function and purpose behind a letter of introduction still remains. When you write a letter of recommendation, you are endorsing the subject's qualifications, skills, and capabilities. And, yes, there is a potential downside to this, which will be discussed later.

To provide an overview of this book and narrow your focus on the sections you need most, you will examine the professional letter of recommendation written for individuals applying to a job opening; the academic letter of recommendation for individual applying to schools, internships, or scholarships; and the networking letter of recommendation written for the purpose of expanding or strengthening your professional network.

The Professional Letter

The professional letter of recommendation is defined as a letter written for someone looking to be hired by a new company or promoted internally to a new position. You might be asked to write this type of letter of recommendation for someone you went to school with, a business associate or colleague, a direct report, or even a manager. You could even be asked to write this kind of letter for someone you have not worked with but have known for a significant period of time.

The first thing to understand about writing a professional letter of recommendation is that you are – generally speaking – addressing the person's ability to do a job and/or perform in a work setting. You should not speak about the person's abilities that you aren't familiar with, but highlight the professional skills that person has demonstrated.

For example, a direct report shouldn't be about a manager's ability to manage a budget or payroll if he or she isn't privy to that information. Instead, the direct report should focus on the manager's ability to keep an operation or project running smoothly, give clear instruction, help solve issues, and provide team mentorship.

Another example includes that a business associate should not speak outside of his/her area of contact for the person they are recommending. Therefore, if your experience with the person is on a client/supplier level, speak about the skills you have witnessed. Don't talk about how the person interacts with co-workers if you have no knowledge on that front. Instead, speak about the negotiating process, how well they delivered on contract specifications, and customer-service experience.

Remember, you are probably not the only person who is writing a letter of recommendation for the candidate. When each letter states the candidate's strengths from an individual's point-of-view, a strong picture is painted for the reader. There is no need to oversell the person; just promote the great quality are familiar with.

The Academic Letter

This letter is usually written for a student's acceptance into an institute of higher education (i.e. college) or used for someone seeking an advanced degree beyond his or her bachelor's degree. Other sections in this book also cover letters used for internships, scholarships, and fellowships.

These letters can profoundly impact someone's academic and professional future as well as his or her ability to pay for education. The letters are important and a little more varied. Rather than just speaking about the person's ability to do a job, you need to address their ability to take on a challenge and succeed.

Each person who writes a letter of recommendation used for academic purposes might not be familiar with the student's grades or academic qualifications. That's okay because an admissions board considers other qualities besides grades. They also want to know if the person possesses leadership qualities, is well rounded, and will contribute to the student body. This is particularly true of advanced degrees.

When a person is seeking admittance into a graduate program, the admissions board is looking for individuals who will enrich the learning experience of their students and could potentially teach undergraduates. This requires highlighting skills sets that make it clear that the candidate will not just excel academically but also as being a part of the program.

The Networking Letter

While most letters you will write are discussed in the two sections above, it's important to review another letter form that could prove useful to your professional development, as well as the person who requests it of you.

A networking letter of recommendation is written when you want to introduce one associate to another. It is less formal than the letters in the first two sections; the tone is more conversational. You might write this letter for someone who another associate would enjoy meeting or perhaps hold an interview with.

This is an interview where you meet with someone of interest within your industry and ask him or her general questions about the industry and/or company. Bring several copies of your resume to the interview, and ask the person to pass them along to companies looking for employees. This is a very effective networking tool that may earn you a job in the future.

A networking interview needs to start off right, so this is where the first type of letter comes in. In this scenario, the letter of recommendation should be written more like a reference letter, which resembles an introduction rather than 'stamp-of-approval' content. However, you still want to write very positive statements about the person and encourage the reader to schedule an interview.

A cousin to this letter would be a networking letter for a job seeker. Again, you are not necessarily putting a strong rubber stamp on the candidate, but you are letting a friend of yours know that an associate of yours is qualified and interested in an available position. Before you send a letter like this, make sure you firmly believe this person will be a good candidate for the position; or else, you risk vouching for a terrible worker.

Always introduce people through online networking sites such as LinkedIn™. People have the opportunity to see if any of your connections work at a company or in a field that interests them. They can even ask you to introduce the person via LinkedIn.

Before you introduce people randomly, make sure you know both individuals well enough to initiate the introduction. While networking is profitable for you in the present and especially in the future, make sure you don't pester any contacts that could serve you well down the road. If someone asks you for an introduction, put some thought into it before you act.

Chapter 2

When (and How) to Say No

Again, it is important to reiterate how a mediocre letter of recommendation can hurt a person's candidacy for a job or academic program. The reader expects a letter of recommendation to be a strong endorsement of a person's capabilities and skills. If you produce a poor letter, then you could eliminate that person from consideration.

There are several things you should consider when you decide rather or not you decide to write a letter of recommendation. And there are several reasons why **you should say no**.

Do not agree to write a letter of recommendation if you cannot emphatically endorse a candidate.

Regardless of your opinion of a person's capabilities, if they list you as a reference or ask for a recommendation letter, don't say yes if you do not feel comfortable saying something positive in the letter. Since standard procedure for listing someone as a reference is cordially asking him or her first, hopefully no one gives out your contact information without checking with you. If you get blind-sided by a call, be honest and let the person know later on that you do not want that to happen again.

The primary focus of this book is not about verbal references, but letters of recommendation. Since you cannot write a letter without agreeing to do it, **do not write a bad letter on purpose**. There is no need to purposefully sabotage someone's job/academic pursuits, and you could subject yourself to potential legal ramifications.

While it can be difficult to win a defamation case, you probably do not want to put yourself in that situation. If the subject of your letter learns that he/she would have been hired, accepted, or given a raise if you had written a good letter, then he/she might have a case for damages. Yes, they would have to prove that you knowingly wrote false statements, but why take the risk? If you cannot say something positive about a person, politely decline to write the letter.

Do not write a letter of recommendation if you do not know enough about the person to adequately endorse them.

Sometimes people – students in particular – are not really sure who to ask for a letter of recommendation. They might ask a college professor who seems nice but can barely remember them. If you can only write a vague letter for that person, explain why you are not the best person to endorse him or her and perhaps find someone better suited for the task.

Remember that some of the things you will need to cover in a letter of recommendation include an evaluation of a person's work ethic, ability to meet deadlines, ability to perform under pressure, how well this person works with others, or in what type of environment the person excels. It is not a good idea to put anything in a letter that you cannot back up during a phone call. Therefore, if you need to decline because you do not know the candidate well enough, please do so. It would be better for him/her to seek a different reference than for you to write a bad one.

Do not agree to write a letter of recommendation if you do not have time.

Many academic institutions have deadlines for submissions and require letters of recommendations to be mailed or emailed directly from the writer. In instances like this, a person cannot ask for a letter from you that they can use and reuse. Even employers might make this same kind of request. If you do not have the time to write a powerful letter in the timeframe a person needs the task completed, do not add this to your never-ending, to-do list. Just tell the person you lack the time right now but he or she can come to you next time.

Note to Applicants

When you consider asking someone for a letter of recommendation, think in advance how well the person knows you. Consider if the person will have something positive to say about you and what character traits, skills, and abilities he or she will be able to endorse about you. Finally, be sure to tell the person, if he or she is too busy to write the letter, that you understand. This should provide the writer with an 'easy out' and ensure that you receive high-quality letters of recommendation.

Chapter 3

What to Know Before You Write a Letter

O nce you have decided to write a letter of recommendation, there is a certain amount of materials you need to do. This information should be provided to you by the recipient of the letter, but if they have been derelict in their duties, ask for the following:

Letter Rules and/or Guidelines

Letters of recommendations may or may not be required for an applicant. Often, they just something serve the applicant well in professional pursuits or for higher education applications and can be sent to multiple institutions.

However, there are times when letters of recommendations need to follow very specific guidelines such as content, deadlines, and methods of submission. If the letter needs to be mailed in a sealed envelope by July 1st, you need to make note of those requirements and adhere to them if you agree to write the letter.

Note to Applicants

If your letters of recommendation need to be submitted by a certain date and in a certain format, provide the person you are asking to write the letter with as much assistance as possible. For example, if the letter needs to be sent by mail to a specific person/department, provide a pre-addressed envelope for the writer. Also, make sure you give the writer plenty of lead-time when asking him or her to meet a specific date. A week's notice is likely insufficient. Ask the potential writer a few weeks before the due date and follow-up in just enough time that he or she can still easily meet the timeframe you need.

Additionally, ask at least one extra person for a letter in this instance (If the application asks for three, you should request a letter from four individuals.) just in case one of your writers fails to deliver or gets their letter in the mail late. Be thankful that they took the time to write letter of recommendations, so don't become stressed out with people who are doing you a favor.

Recipient of the Letter

While some job candidates and school applicants will ask for letters they can use for multiple applications, others will need them addressed to specific hiring managers or committee members. In these instances, you will want to address your letter to an individual, not a generic recipient (i.e. Dear Sarah Marshall or Dear Hiring Manager).

Even when you do not have a specific person to address, you can still customize your letter to companies or schools if you know the focus of the individual's job or academic pursuits. This is important because you might mention certain achievements above others if you know what the reader will find the most interesting or valid.

Job Description or School/Program Information

In continuation of the concept above, if the subject of the letter can provide you a job description or details about the university or program the applicant wants to attend, you can write a more targeted letter. In these instances, select key words from the job description or program website to plug into your letter. These descriptions can also give you guidance in what achievements or qualifications you can note about the subject of the letter.

After you have acquired this information, begin drafting the letter and planning what you are going to say about the recipient. If you determine through this information gathering process that you will be unable to meet a deadline or some other rule for submission, inform the person immediately so they can ask someone else to write the letter.

Note to Applicants

Provide the person(s) you ask for a letter with this information from the start. You can also provide them with your resume, cover letter, and other notes regarding your qualifications, career progression, and achievements. In an academic setting, tell a professor what class you were enrolled in and the semester in which you completed the course. If you still have papers or assignments you completed for the class, ask if the professor wants to review them to refresh himself/herself on your work. If you have written a statement of purpose, provide the writer with a copy. Remember, the more information you provide the writer, the better letter he or she can assemble for you.

Chapter 4

Writing a Strong Letter Part One: Structure, Format, & Grammar

Writing a letter of recommendation is not as simple as writing a loosely written email. In today's world, communication purely takes place through emailing and other shorthand messages; the art of writing letters is slowing slipping away. While you might send your letter of recommendation via email, many of the points addressed in this book are based on the assumption that you will print and mail the letter "the old fashion way."

Letter Components

If you cannot remember your grammar/middle-school training on how to prepare a letter, this chapter reviews the basic elements of letter writing, starting with the main components of a letter:

- Header
- Address/Salutation
- Opening paragraph
- Body
- Closing paragraph
- Signature

Header

A business letter is written with a header that includes your name, phone number, and email address as well as a business or physical address if you choose to include one. (The physical address is optional.) Since this is a business-communications letter, the information you include should present a positive professional image.

For example, you might want to list your work phone or a cell phone number rather than your home listing to ensure you are the one who answers the call. You should also provide an email address that is professional (firstname.lastname@email.com) rather than one that is overly personal (sexybeast@email.com).

If you do not already have a letterhead prepared, see the examples below:

SAMATHA ROBERTSON

Sacramento, California 97844 | 966-555-7653 | slrobertson73@xxx.com

MARK WASHINGTON, OPERATIONS MANAGER

Major Telecom Company, Atlanta, GA 47379
Work: (706) 555-8373 | markwashington68@hotmail.xxx

ALEXANDRA HAYES

Vice-President of Retail Organization | Orlando, FL 34789
Work: 407-555-1234 | ahayes@comcast.xxx

Address/Salutation

Your letter should be addressed to the appropriate person, whether this is a hiring manager, human resources manager, or director of admissions. This information should be provided to you by the subject of the letter. Again, since this is a business communications, it requires a full business address and appropriate salutation. See the examples below:

Example:

Mr. Ben Nobles
General Sales Manager
Dollar General
1254 North Atlanta Blvd.
Jacksonville FL 34875

Dear Mr. Nobles:

Ms. Jennifer Smith
Director of Admissions
University of Florida
Gainesville, FL 34875

Dear Ms. Smith:

Opening Paragraph

The opening paragraph of your letter should state your purpose for sending the letter; you should include the name of the requestor and explain your connection to them. You can also briefly setup what the body of your letter is going to support in detail. This statement should be two or three short lines.

Examples:

"At the request of Jessica Long, I am writing to recommend her for the position of sales manager. I have worked with Jessica for five years at Company Name and have found her to be an excellent leader and dynamic sales professional."

"It is my great pleasure to recommend to you Jason Franklin for the position of project manager. As a long-time professional associate, I have worked with Jason on several assignments at Company Name. I can attest to his professional skills and leadership ability."

> *"I am writing this letter at the request of Samantha Smith who is applying to your business school. I have been Samantha's soccer coach for five years and instructed her in biology. I can speak well to both her academic skills and her work ethic."*
>
> *"I am writing to you today on behalf of John Kelley who is a candidate from your graduate program. Having instructed him in several upper level courses, I can attest to his research abilities and classroom contributions."*

Combining your introduction as the purpose of the letter and how you know the candidate, you may want to include your qualifications to evaluate the person's credentials or skills. The stronger your qualifications, the more impact the letter could make on the reader.

Examples:

> *"I am writing this letter at the request of Julia Smith who is applying for your inside sales position. As a regional manager of Company Name, I hire and train dozens of sales personnel each year."*
>
> *"I am pleased to write this letter on behalf of Sarah Jones, an applicant to your fall program. As a former entrepreneur and Sarah's business teacher and High School Name, I believe she will make an excellent addition to your program."*

Body

Generally speaking, keep your letter of recommendation to one page. This means the body of your letter will likely be three to four paragraphs. To ensure your letter has the greatest impact, you should select a few key highlights to point out about the subject and focus on those. Assume the recipient has asked several people to write letters, and rather than cover everything in your letter alone, you can speak about what you know best.

The paragraphs in the body of your letter can include personal stories that you feel communicate the value of the person you are recommending or bullet points that quickly breakdown what are the person's key characteristics. This book will cover both strategies in greater detail and give examples of both.

Closing Paragraph

The closing paragraph should reiterate your recommendation or endorsement of the candidate. You should also answer any additional questions the reader has for you regarding the subject of the letter.

Examples:

"In closing, I reiterate the positive contribution I believe James will bring to your operation. If I can provide you with any additional information, please feel free to contact me at your convenience."

"I strongly believe that Susan will be a positive additional to your program. Her passion for the subject matter and commitment to research will prove beneficial to your faculty and students. Please feel free to contact me if you have any additional questions regarding Susan or my experience with her."

Signature

When signing your letter, you will want to use a typed and handwritten signature. Make sure they match your name as is presented in the header of your letter.

Formatting Elements

One key element of professional writing is consistency in font, format, and presentation. Once you select a font, you must stick with it throughout your letter. Use the same font size throughout the document. Margins should be consistent on the top and bottom of the letter and on the left and right sides of the page. While writing your letter of recommendation, there are several formatting elements you can use to improve presentation and impact, but the key is consistency.

Font Style

When selecting your font, the easiest thing to do is to use a common font for Microsoft Word that most people will be able to open and read with their Word programs. These can include the following:

Tahoma
Verdana
Arial
Bookman Old Style
Times New Roman
Calibri

In the most updated versions of Microsoft Word, 'Calibri 11' is the default setting. The other fonts listed are very common as well, particularly Arial and Times New Roman. Avoid using customized or third-party fonts. Even if you are printing the letter to mail it, you will want to provide a copy to the person you are writing the recommendation for, and he or she will need the document saved in an accessible font. Additionally, if you transmit the file electronically and the recipient's computer does not have that same font installed, the computer will make a "best guess" at the font, which could lead to disastrous results in terms of how the formatting will appear.

Serif or Sans Serif

If you have researched fonts, you might know a bit about the **serifs** versus **sans serifs** debate. Confusion on serifs versus sans serifs exists, and recommendations on both ends are present. (The font list above includes both types of font.)

Before we attempt to answer the "to serif or not to serif" question, it is important to define the serif. It is the little decorative stoke that extends for the letters in a type set. It can be in the form of a tail, sharp or blunt, decorative or plain. The serifs appear on both upper and lower case and impact numbers as well. Each serif font has a style for this mark that makes them unique. From the list above, Times New Roman is the most common of the serif fonts.

Sans serif (without serif) means that the letters and numbers are written without the strokes at the end of the letters. The character edges may be sharp or rounded, but they lack the decorative add on. The most common sans serif font is Arial and the new default font for Microsoft Word - Calibri.

Some will claim that serif fonts are hard to read while others claim the opposite. One type of thinking states that san serif fonts are informal and that business writing should lean toward the more classical font type. The simple truth is that there are common fonts that fall into both categories, so use the one with which you are most comfortable or like the best. As long as it is a commonly used font – serif or no – it should work fine for your letter writing endeavors.

Font Size

Fonts that are formatted in the same font size can still take up more or less room on the page. You may remember from your days of writing essays in high school or college that various fonts allowed you to better align your paper with the minimum or maximum page range you were given for an assignment. Professors who are aware of this might dictate the font choices and sizes you are allowed to employ. For those who don't, many students use a font that took up more space on the page or increased their font size by one point to extend the length of their content.

When writing your letter of recommendation, if you are finding it difficult to fit what you want to say onto one page, you can practice the opposite of what most students do. Rather than expand your content, you can shrink it. You can reduce from 12 point font down to 11 or at times 10 depending on the font type. You may use Times New Roman instead of Arial. Even in the same size, Times takes up less space on the page.

Just make sure you do not use a font that is too small. Your letter of recommendation needs to be legible. Some smaller font types to avoid might include Garamond or Perpetual, both of which tend to run significantly smaller than the common fonts listed above.

Generally speaking, it is best to use a font size that is between 10 and12 depending on the font type you have selected. If you stay within that, then your letter of recommendation should still be easily visible.

It is important to note that you want your document to be easily read when it transmits or prints out. People tend to put documents they send electronically on a setting higher than 100 percent, which enlarges the font they selected to make it more legible but also causes the page to take up more space on the screen. Reset everything to 100 percent to get a feel for what the document is supposed to look like. Additionally, this setting will not help you when printing the letter.

Margins

While changing font style and size can help you save space in your letter of recommendation, there are other formatting options you can use to keep the document to one page. Margins do not necessarily need to remain at one inch on all sides, which is the Microsoft Word default setting. You can select the 'Page Layout' tab and the 'Margin' section to alter this setting. Just go down to "Custom Margins" and reduce the space dedicated to the top and bottom margins and/or left and right margins. You can reduce them to .8 or .7 on all sides if need be, but keep the top and bottom margins even and the left and right margins even to protect the visual evenness of the page.

Single Spacing

You probably know to "single space" your document, but what you might not realize is that Microsoft Word no longer defaults to a single space setting. The default on Microsoft Word is the 1.15 line space setting. This allows some space to appear between each line without the "double space" appearance.

To save space, select your paragraph option and under the "Indents and Spacing" tab select single spacing and check the box that says "Do not add space between paragraphs of the same style." Also under the spacing option, make sure the "before" and "after" boxes are set to zero.

If you follow these recommendations, you can ensure your document will save as much space as possible between lines and paragraphs. Don't use the header option to type your contact information into the document as this can take up more space than needed in the document.

Mailed Letters vs. Emailed Letters

While some letters of recommendations will need to be mailed and postmarked by a specific date, others will be sent by email. Because of the differences in these two forms of communications, you should make note of a couple of rules to follow when using electronic or print mail.

When sending a letter by mail, you should print it on high-quality, watermark paper with a full letterhead. Your letterhead should include your first and last name, email address, and phone number. It should also include standard letter components such as date, name of the addressee, salutation, opening paragraph, several supporting paragraphs, a closing, and signature. These elements are reviewed in greater detail in other sections of the book and several examples are included in the latter chapters.

A printed letter of recommendation will make a better impression on a reader, but there may be times when it is appropriate to send your letter via email. In that case, you may abbreviate the letter to include the name of the addressee, salutation, introductory paragraph, support paragraph, and closing statements. When tying your name on email, you should make sure your signature includes contact information (including phone). There are a few samples in the back of the book of how the same letter can be formatted for print or email.

Paragraphs vs. Bullets

When writing a letter of recommendation, presentation can be almost as important as content. One of the key elements of presentation is whether you will write the letter using a paragraph only format or if you will incorporate bullets into your document. Each style choice has some advantages, and you should select the format that best suits the information you want to convey as well as your personality.

If you want to relay a few highlights about the candidate quickly or if you are the kind of person who prefers brevity, a bulleted format might work best for you. On the other hand, if you know the person really well and/ or have a great deal you can say about the candidate or a specific job the candidate worked on, you might want to use a paragraph format to facilitate better "story telling." You may even find you prefer one style for one candidate's letter and the other for a different candidate.

Paragraphs for Story Telling

The two common ways you can format your paragraphs is to use a block or indented-paragraph format. Both are acceptable and your decision will likely come down to your personal preference.

In the block format, every element of the letter is flush with the left margin, including the date, signature lines, and opening lines of each new paragraph. In the indented-paragraph format, the date and signature lines will be indented four inches from the left margin and the opening line of each paragraph will be indented one-quarter inch or one-half inch depending on preference.

Examples of each format are contrasted on the following pages:

Indented Paragraph Format:

GORDAN R. "ROBERT" JONES

7849 North Center Street   Office: (489) 555-9899
West Bend, WI 58939   Mobile: (478) 555-9878

January 3, 2015

Dear Jane Smith,

I am writing you to recommend Sarah Longfellow for admissions to your university's school of business. I have had the pleasure of coaching Sarah in soccer for four years and instructing her in Spanish her freshman and sophomore year of high school.

Sarah has displayed a very strong commitment to both her athletic and academic pursuits. This passion and effort has lead her soccer team (of which she is co-captain) to finish third and second in the state the last two years while Sarah has earned a top five ranking in a 300+ member graduating class. Sarah is an enthusiastic, hard-working, and kind student. She frequently goes the extra mile to help her classmates or teammates achieve their goals.

I know Sarah is also deeply involved in her church and community organizations. She volunteers in summer soccer camps to help teach children the basics of soccer skills and teamwork. She has also travelled on church-sponsored mission trips to Spanish-speaking countries where she helped build homes and honed her Spanish skills.

Sarah has expressed a strong interest in pursuing international business studies at university while continuing to strengthen and expanding her foreign language abilities. I believe you will find her to be a highly successful member of your student body and recommend you accept her application. If I can provide you with any additional information, please contact me at the phone and email address listed above. Thank you for your time.

Regards,

Robert Jones

Block Paragraph Format:

Steve W "Will" Robinson

555-555-5555 | 7849 North Center Street, West Bend, WI 58939 | steverobinson3357@email.com

January 5, 2015

Ms. Janie Brown
Atlantic Industries
jbrown@atlanticindustries.xxx

Dear Ms. Brown:

Helen Jones has requested that I write to you on her behalf to recommend her for your graduate program in human resources management. I hired Helen after she graduated from University of State with her bachelor's degree in psychology and education, and she has proven a valuable training asset.

Helen began her time with us by developing and leading new-hire orientations for dozens of employees at a time. After completing several professional development courses on adult-learning methodology, she transitioned into our corporate university. Since then she has created two new classes and led a half dozen others in classroom and on-line webinar settings.

I find Helen to be an excellent teacher and trainer, so when she came to me and said she wanted to complete her master's degree to transition in management career path, I fully supported the idea. You will find Helen an excellent addition to your program and potential source of real-world experience for her fellow students.

I plan on employing Helen part-time while she pursues her education, but will adjust her work load as needed to ensure she gets the most out of her academic endeavors. If I can be of any additional assistance in your consideration of her application, please let me know. I can be reached at the phone and email listed above. Thank you for your time.

Sincerely,

Will Robinson

Bullets for Short Points

Using bullets in the body of your letter of recommendation makes the letter more readable. It is also an excellent way to grab the attention of your reader and quickly convey information to them that you find to be most important. The reader's eyes are immediately drawn to the bullet points, and he or she understands the essence of your message better if he or she gives your letter of recommendation a quick scan.

A sample letter using the bulleted format is presented on the next page:

RENA LONG

555-555-5555 | Street Address, City, State, Zip | renalong123@email.com

(Date)

Mr. (Ms.) _____

Title

(Company)

(Address 1)

(Address 2)

Dear Mr. (Ms.) _____

I am writing to you on behalf of Ashley Hale, recommending her for admissions to your school of business for the MBA program. Ashley worked for me at XYZ Corporation while she was earning her undergraduate and has developed into a fine marketing manager over the last two years since she joined us full-time.

Ashley's creativity and use of print, broadcast, and digital media has helped drive a 15 percent sales growth over the last two years. Now she wants to earn her MBA so that she can gain a deeper understanding of business management and begin an executive track with the company. I fully support her in these efforts. Please consider the following points about Ashley's work:

- She manages multiple projects well by prioritizing the most important tasks and creatively addressing issues when they arise to ensure projects stay on-track and on-budget.

- She works well in cross-functional environments and has taken on the task of selecting and mentoring a summer intern since she went to work full-time in our creative department.

- She is fully bilingual in Spanish and English and often volunteers to work with our teams in Mexico to ensure our marketing material communicates effectively with Spanish-speaking consumers.

Ashley maintained a high GPA while working for me and obtaining her undergraduate degree. I fully support her effort to complete her MBA now and will accommodate her schedule however I need to so that she can place her studies first. If you need any additional information regarding Ashley, please feel free to contact me at the phone number or email listed above.

Sincerely,

Rena Long

Side-by-Side Comparisons

To understand how these two formats contrast effectively and which one might be best for you, consider how the two formats convey the identical information listed below:

Paragraph

Danielle shows a great love for literature as the president of student book club at our school. You would think advanced students get enough reading assignments during class, but a handful of our students tackle additional books as a group – discussing and dissecting them at length. While this is admirable on its own, the greatest thing this group does is perform readings for pre-school and elementary-aged children at our local library.

Danielle and her friends pick several books each week and read the stories to the children, assigning special voices to each of the characters. They often pick one or two children from the audience and ask them to read along with them. They are helping bring these books alive for these children and creating what I hope will be a life-long love for literature in these young minds.

In addition to her love for reading, Danielle is a talented writer herself. She works on our student newspaper and has written several creative pieces for the newspaper and my class as well. I bring this up not because Danielle will focus her studies in this area, but to call out her excellent communication skills that I know will benefit her in college.

Bullets

Please consider the following points regarding Danielle's candidacy:

- She has demonstrated a great love of literature as the president of the student book club and facilitated group discussions at monthly meetings.

- Mentors and reads for pre-school and elementary aged children at the local library.
- Writes news and creative pieces for publications in the student paper.

Writing Guidelines

As mentioned early in the book, the letter of recommendation can prove invaluable to someone's job or college application, therefore, it is important that your letter be professional, high quality, and represent the applicant well. This means that it must be error free, well written, and strongly present the applicant's abilities and/or skills.

If you are the type of person who is uncomfortable with strong statements, you might want to get some help in this letter writing task. A letter of recommendation is not the place for a timid on mild endorsement. The reader will be expecting a positive letter from you; if you dance around the recommendation, it might leave a question in the reader's mind to the qualifications of the candidate.

While you do not want to exaggerate the recipient's qualifications, strengths, or positives, a letter of recommendation is a "sale" or "marketing" tool that you do not want to soft peddle. More than anything, you do not want to bore the reader or lose their attention. Brevity should assist in that endeavor, but so will other writing methodologies. Consider the following:

Write in active voice:

Active voice is more dynamic than passive voice and generally the preferred style for all writing assignments. The difference comes from how the subject of the sentence relates to the action being expressed by the verb. Consider:

In sentences written in <u>active voice</u>, the subject of the sentence <u>performs</u> the action expressed in the verb used.

> *The cat scratched the little girl.*
>
> *Michelle will present her recommendation at the board meeting.*

In sentences written in <u>passive voice</u>, the subject of the sentence <u>receives</u> the action being expressed by the verb.

> *The little girl was scratched by the cat.*
>
> *Recommendations will be presented by Michelle at the board meeting.*

In a letter of recommendation, using active voice communicates to the reader that the subject of your letter performed tasks and accomplishments rather than being the subject of those actions. This is important because ultimately your reader wants to know what the candidate can **DO** – not what they can participate in or be involved in or even have done to them. Additionally, active voice is a tighter form of writing than passive voice where you use fewer words to say the same thing.

Write in simple tense:

Along with writing in active voice, you need to be aware of what tense you are using when you write. You are probably conjuring up bad memories of diagramming sentences as you read this thinking that you barely survived high school grammar – there is no way you are going to remember all that information now.

The good news is that my advice is not that complicated. For letter writing, you should use the simple tense whenever possible. This will allow you to keep your word count (and letter length) down while keeping your sentences dynamic.

Consider the differences between the following examples:

> *Susan has a great passion for teaching.*
>
> **Susan is a passionate instructor.**
>
> *Philip has demonstrated strong budgeting skills and resourcefulness on several projects.*
>
> **Philip infuses astute budgeting and resourcefulness into his approach for project management.**

It is vitally important that you use every opportunity to shorten your message in a letter of recommendation without losing impact. Writing in the simple tense and eliminating words like "have" when appropriate is an excellent way to achieve that goal.

Use assertive language:

Avoid using phrases like "I believe" or "I think" in your letter of recommendation. You do not want to leave the reader with the impression that you are unsure of your assessment of the subject of the letter. State firmly what you have to say about the candidate.

In doing this, use action words in your letter of recommendation. You will want to use action verbs for you part of the letter (such as "I endorse…" or "Rachael impressed me by…") and for the candidate's achievements. Action verbs communicate achievements, qualifications, and skills. The table below lists several action verbs you might want to use in your letter. A longer table is included in Chapter 15: Quick Guides for Letter Writing)

Action words:

Acted	Created	Generated	Produced
Advanced	Customized	Hired	Projected
Analyzed	Debugged	Identified	Promoted
Approved	Decreased	Implemented	Provided
Assigned	Demonstrated	Improved	Published
Audited	Designed	Increased	Purchased
Authored	Developed	Initiated	Recruited
Automated	Directed	Installed	Reduced
Balanced	Edited	Instructed	Researched
Budgeted	Educated	Integrated	Restructured
Built	Eliminated	Interviewed	Saved
Collaborated	Enabled	Launched	Solved
Communicated	Enhanced	Led	Specified
Completed	Established	Managed	Standardized
Composed	Evaluated	Marketed	Streamlined
Conducted	Executed	Negotiated	Strengthened
Consolidated	Expedited	Organized	Supervised
Contributed	Facilitated	Planned	Tested
Converted	Forecasted	Presented	Trained
Coordinated	Grew	Processed	Wrote

Note that these action verbs are listed in past tense because, in most cases, you will be talking about something the person has already done. If you need to write about something they are currently working on or pursuing, you can change the action verbs to present tense.

The goal of your letter of recommendation is to say as much as you can in as few words as possible.

Make your Message Concise

Even when limiting yourself to a one-page letter of recommendation, it is still possible to ramble in the three to five paragraphs allotted. The goal of your letter of recommendation is to say as much as you can in as few words as possible. In the interest of doing that, consider the following recommendations:

Eliminate unnecessary words

Adjectives and adverbs serve a very important role in day-to-day language and writing. They are wonderful ways to project personality and flare into your work. For that purpose, they have a place in your letter of recommendation; however, you must be selective in how you use them.

Words like 'greatly', 'really', and 'very' are unnecessary in a letter of recommendation. If the meaning of your words would not be altered by eliminating an adjective or adverb, it may be best to cut the extra word. However, if the use of an adjective or adverb adds to the message you are trying to convey, keep it in.

Additionally, there are times when people use adjectives in their writing to convey meaning where actual results would tell a better story. If you are using an adjective to explain that an achievement was very good, it might be better to quantify the achievement in some manner. Dollar figures tend to make the greatest impact, but you can also use percentages or other metrics to explain the benefit of the work, skills, or accomplishments you are describing.

Consider the sentences below:

> *Jane Smith made a very strong contribution to the development and launch of a great new product line that received a lot of positive praise for being one of our greatest products ever.*
>
> ***Jane played an integral role in the development and launch of a new product line that was rated as best-in-class per corporate metrics for time-to-market, customer reception, and initial sales.***

In the first sentence, the writer used "unnecessary" words to convey meaning that was not backed up by performance metrics or quantifiable figures. The second sentence does not tell you the new product line was "great" but rather explains why it was top-rated.

Now consider the following sentences where unnecessary words are cut out:

> *Paul managed a very important project for our company where he oversaw the implementation of process improvements that extremely enhanced our manufacturing productivity and really, really lowered costs.*
>
> ***Paul managed the implementation of process improvements that enhanced manufacturing productivity and lowered costs.***

Please note that the second sentence conveys relatively the same meaning as the first without the fluffy language or unnecessary words. If the writer wanted to strengthen the second sentence more, he/she could mention how much productivity was enhanced or costs were lowered. Consider:

> ***Paul managed the implementation of process improvements that enhanced manufacturing productivity 20 percent and lowered costs $200K per cycle.***

While it is clear that numbers tell a better story than a sentence without them, do not be tempted to use flowery language to compensate for not having numbers. Read the first two sentences again and you will realize the first does not really make a greater impact than the second, but it uses a lot more space to tell the same tale.

Eliminate run-on sentences

Your letter of recommendation will be more effective when it is written with short, punchy sentences. Run-on sentences should be completely eliminated. By definition, a run-on sentence is when two independent clauses (a group of words that include a subject and verb) are run together without a conjunction and/or punctuation between them. Not only are run-on sentences grammatically incorrect and space killers, they also make a letter more difficult to read.

> A good target for your sentence length is between 15-25 words. If it is longer than that, find a way to break it up.

Additionally, if you are talking too much about one specific point, you will miss the opportunity to address others for lack of space. A good target for your sentence length is between 15-25 words. If it is longer than that, find a way to break it up.

Consider the following before and after examples of how to take a run-on sentence and tighten it into short, impactful statement.

> *Julian was very supportive of the sales team he was proactive in solving technical problems for the sales team and he would conduct the technical aspects of sales presentations.*
>
> ***Julian supported the sales team by conducting the technical aspects of presentations and proactively solving technical issues.***
>
> *Michael is an exceptional chef and I have never seen someone design such a well-received menu selection for restaurant guests and deliver such quality food presentations for all the diners.*
>
> ***Michael is an exceptional chef who designed well-received menu selections and provided diners with high-quality food presentations.***

In both instances, the second sentence is easier to read and conveys the point of the matter better than the first. Also, in each example, the second sentence is shorter than the first which will allow you to cover more information in a smaller amount of space. Ultimately, this should help you engage the reader more and communicate your points better.

Eliminate tacit information

Tacit information is that which is implied or already known. There might not be a lot of tacit information in your letter, but be sure to edit it with this guideline in mind. Examples of tacit information could include labeling your phone number with the word "phone" or stating obvious facts within the letter itself.

Consider the difference between these two sentences:

> *John Smith has asked me to write a letter of recommendation for his application to your law program.*
>
> **I am writing to you on behalf of John Smith who applying to your law program.**

In the first sentence, the writer has stated something the reader can conclude on their own. After all, you would not be writing the letter if the person had not asked you to. On the other hand, the second line serves as a solid introductory sentence without communicating tacit information.

The space saving difference between the first sentence and the second is not more than a few words, but it can make a large difference over the course of the entire letter. Remember, the goal of the letter is to make the highest impact with the fewest words.

Never, ever be redundant

You have a limited amount of space to convey your message to your reader – do not waste it. Consider the differences in the follow examples:

> *Mary Sue is a very enthusiastic leader who brings a lot of energy to her work and energizes her whole team on difficult assignments as a result.*
>
> **Mary Sue is a very enthusiastic leader who brings a lot of energy to her work and energizes her whole team on difficult assignments as a result.**

> *Paul is a very astute planner and project manager. He provides management that allows his teams to deliver projects early at reduced costs. He manages client budgets well and always saves them money.*
>
> *Paul demonstrates a firm ability to expedite projects and lower costs, saving his clients significant amounts of money through astute planning and management.*

Eliminating redundant words saves space and conveys your message more effectively. Besides tightening up your message, you should also avoid using the same word several times throughout your document. Try employing synonyms when possible to eliminate redundancy. See the synonym list in Chapter 15 for some common words that you might use frequently in a letter and would need to employ synonyms for to avoid redundant wording.

Avoid spill over words

When going over your final edit, avoid "widowed words." These widowed words occur when you write a sentence and the last word of that sentence spills over to the second (or third) line by itself. In most cases, rewording the sentence can eliminate the widowed word and save space on your page. When that fails, you can adjust your margins or font dimensions to bring the word back onto the same line as the rest of the sentence. Review the synonym list above or use the 'SHIFT-F7' thesaurus tool in Microsoft Word.

If you need to adjust the formatting on your page, please review the section on page setup/formatting for hints at changing margin spacing and font dimensions to save space.

Spell it out and Avoid Company Jargon:

The vast majority of these writing guidelines are about saving space and saying things in a succinct manner. However, there is an exception to this strategy, and that is the use of acronyms and abbreviations. Due to texting, Twitter, and other social media platforms, acronyms and abbreviations have become a language of their own, but remember that formal business communications, such as a letter of recommendation, is not a place for shorthand or short cuts.

Even if your letter of recommendation is written for someone in your career field who understands common acronyms, be cautious and spell everything out. As a professional resume writer, I will admit to using some wide-spread business acronyms in the documents I create. However, I have learned that no matter how "common" I think an acronym is there are still readers who might not understand it.

Company jargon and abbreviations are even worse. There are times when my clients use abbreviations so common to them that they do not even realize that someone outside their company has no idea what they are talking about. Additionally, there are times when acronyms mean different things to different people or different things in different companies/industries. Consider:

> *SDLC = Software Development Lifecycle OR Systems*
> *   Development Lifecycle*
> *USC = University of South Carolina OR University of*
> *   Southern California*

Again, to ensure you meaning is being properly received, **it is best to spell things out and use common terminology**. However, if there is still an acronym you want to use, review the following chart of common business acronyms and their meanings to ensure you are on the same page as your reader.

Common Business Acronym Chart

A/P A/R	Accounts Payable Accounts Receivable	Accounts that need to be paid Payments to be received
B2B	Business to Business	Companies that sell products or services to other companies
B2C	Business to Consumer	Companies that sell products or services to individuals
CEO	Chief Executive Officer	Head of a company
CFO	Chief Financial Officer	Head of the financial aspect of a company
COO	Chief Operating Office	Leads the operations aspects of a company
CRM	Customer Relationship Management	System that captures, analyzes, and stores customer data
EBITDA	Earnings before interests, taxes, depreciation, and amortization	A measure of financial performance
GAAP	Generally Accepted Accounting Principles	A framework for financial accounting
HR	Human Resources	The part of an organization that handles hiring, labor law compliance, and other personnel-related functions
IPO	Initial Public Offerings	When a company first sells shares of its stock to the public
NDA	Non-Disclosure Agreement	A contract that ensures confidentiality of information
OEM	Original Equipment Manufacturer	Company that first manufactures a product that will be rebranded and sold by other companies
OTC	Over-the-Counter	Medicines available without a prescription
P&L	Profit and Loss	Accounting report used to outline how revenues and transformed into profits
POS	Point of Sale	Point in a store where checkout occurs
PR	Public Relations	Relating to the public and/or media on behalf of the company
QA/QC	Quality Assurance or Quality Control	Process of ensuring quality for products and services

R&D	Research and Development	Early stage of product or service development
RFQ/ RFP	Request for Quote/ Request for Proposal	Request for bids on a project or service
ROI	Return on Investment	The ratio of money earned relative to money invested
SaaS	Software as a Service	Software developed on the web and accessible via the Internet
TQM	Total Quality Management	Management method that focuses the whole unit on quality
VC	Venture Capital	Financing where owners give up part ownership for capital

Write clean

The presentation or "look" of your letter is about than just formatting; it is also about simple appearance. This means that your letter of recommendation is visually appealing and easy to read, from font choice to paper quality. You will want to avoid things like ink smudges, excessive underlining, and errors. More detailed recommendations include:

Avoid messiness

In those circumstances where you print and mail your letter of recommendation, your document should be pristine.

In my junior year of high school, my American literature instructor insisted that we submit rough drafts of every assignment we turned in. It did not matter if corrections were made on our computers. We were required to print a copy and make it look like we hand-edited it. He once told us to give it to our younger siblings and let them get peanut butter and jelly stains on it if we had to; he wanted a rough draft.

Your readers will not.

A hiring director does not want to see a letter of recommendation that has been crumpled up, dog-eared, has stains, or hand-written corrections.

Your letter should be printed on quality paper if it needs to be mailed directly to the school or company requesting it. You can find business quality, watermarked paper at most stores that sell office supplies. If you are just providing the letter to the person you are writing it about to use and reuse, give it to them in printed and electronic formats and make sure you save the document to your computer files if they need to ask you for it again or ask you to send it directly to one particular employer or admissions board.

Note to Applicants

If you are printing the letters of recommendation yourself, you need to print your letters and résumé on high-quality, watermarked paper. Print only on white or off-white paper.

Do not overdo the formatting.

Using **bold**, *italics*, and <u>underlining</u> can be an effective way to enhance parts of your letter of recommendation. Each choice can help you put specific emphasis on a point you really want to grab the reader's attention. Consider:

- **Administered P& L for $22M in annual revenue and delivered on a plan to increase sales 22 percent** for Company XYZ while developing key strategic relationships with clients such as ABC, 123, and 789.

- Directed a project for transitioning customer web page accounts to new hosting vendor that *resulted in more than $200K annual savings for Company ABC.*

- Defined business specifications for users to <u>improve reporting and save company time and money</u>.

However, it is important not to <u>overuse</u> them individually or collectively, because overuse of them can prove distracting to the reader. Consider the following:

- **Administered P& L for $22M in annual revenue** and <u>delivered on a plan to increase sales 22 percent</u> for Company XYZ while **developing key strategic relationships with clients such as ABC, 123, and 789**.

- **Directed a project for transitioning customer web page accounts to new hosting vendor** that *resulted in <u>more than $200K annual savings for Company ABC</u>*.

- *Defined business specifications for users to <u>improve reporting and save company time and money</u>*.

In the first examples, the formatting choice drew out certain points for the readers. In a document full of the second examples, the reader's eyes might cross and miss the points you wanted to emphasis. Bottom line: You should use these bits of formatting selectively.

Edit and Re-edit

The key to presenting a clean document is editing. You should expect to write a couple of drafts of your letter. While the draft and editing process might take place in one document on your computer, it is a good idea to print it at least once and complete a hand-written edit on the document.

When proof reading, try to take some time between when you finished the draft and when you examined it again for the edit. The break between writing and editing efforts will allow you to see the document with fresh eyes and perhaps catch something you previously missed.

Spell-check and grammar-check through Microsoft Word or search the Internet for a free spell check or grammar check that you can download and use.

Common Grammatical/Word Use Mistakes to Avoid

When writing a strong letter of recommendation – or any business letter – you must exercise proper use of grammar. Even if you think the people on your social networking page who flip out by the misuse of its and it's are nuts, you might want to send them a copy of your letter and ask them to review it for correctness. At the end of the day, writing something well means writing it correctly, and it is imperative that your document be error-free. For a quick guide to avoiding common errors, review the following notes:

Affect/Effect	• Affect is a verb that means to influence. *Your ability to communicate clearly will affect the outcome of the meeting)*
	• Effect is a noun that means result. Think cause and effect. *The cause was the storm; the effect was the fallen building.*

Alot	• This is incorrect. It is always "a lot."
Can't Hardly	• This is incorrect as it is a double negative.
Can not/ Cannot	• Cannot is correct.
Day to Day/ Day-to-Day	• Use hyphen when the phrase is used as a modifier. *He manages day-to-day operations.*
Ensure/Insure	• Ensure means to guarantee. *He ensured the team achieved their growth objectives.* • Insure is used to reference insurance. *The policy insures their vehicle and boat.*
Good/Well	• Good is an adjective that means something is better than average. • Well is used to mean suitable, proper, or healthy.
Imply/Infer	• Imply is to convey meaning to others. • Infer is the meaning you gather from what others are saying/writing.
Irregardless	• Not a word. Regardless is correct.
It's/Its	• It's is a contraction of the words "it is." • Its is a possessive pronoun indicating ownership. *Put the chair over in its place.*
Loose/Lose	• Loose means that something is not tight. • Lose means you have had something taken away from you.
Over/More Than	• Over is spatial or a direction. *The cow jumped over the moon.* • More than is correct for numerals. *She increased sales more than 50 percent.*
Startup/ Start-up	• Startup (one word, not hyphenated) is used to describe a new business venture. • Start-up is correct in UK English spellings.
That/Which	• That is used with essential clauses -- cannot be eliminated without changing the meaning of the sentence. *She implemented a policy that product a 10 percent gain)* • Which is used with nonessential clauses -- can be removed without changing the basic meaning of the sentence. *She implemented a policy, which was used at her previous company, to increase sales 6 percent.*

They're/Their/There	• They're is a contraction of the words "they are." • Their is a possessive pronoun indicating ownership. *Benji is their dog.* • There is an adverb that means "in or at that place." It is used to tell where something is. *The ball is over there.*
Toward/Towards	• Toward is the correct spelling.
Two/Too/To	• Two refers to the number 2. • Too means "in addition to" or "also." *She has four cats and a dog too.* It can also mean more than what should be, very or extremely. *That color is too bright. I am too excited!* • To can serve as a preposition or ad adverb and is more difficult to define. The best rule is to understand the definitions of two and too then you should be safe using to the rest of the time.
Who's/Whose	• Who's is a contraction of the words "who is." • Whose indicates possession. *Whose dog is that? Brandy, whose mother is sick, will not be here today.*
You're/Your	• You're is a contraction of the words "you are." • Your is a possessive pronoun indicating ownership. *Your company. Your car.*

For grammatical guidance beyond these rules, remember that Microsoft Word can run both a spell check and grammar check to help you. There are also several websites where you can look up grammar rules. It is worth the extra effort to ensure your document is mistake-free.

Chapter 5

Writing a Strong Letter Part Two: Content Strategy

Part two of this book examines different types of letters of recommendations and very specific requirements for each letter-writing circumstance. Every letter, whether written by a manager for a current or former employee or by a teacher for a former student, will contain multiple elements and some basic themes. Review this section to make sure your letter covers the big-picture questions you need to answer.

Identify the Purpose of the Letter

In most circumstances, your letter of recommendation will be submitted as part of an application package. However, there may be times when your letter is mailed or sent separately to the hiring manager or admissions board. In either case, you should not assume that the reader will know why they have received this letter from you; therefore, you need to include the following information in the opening paragraph.

Within the first line or two of the letter of recommendation, you should identify why you are writing the letter, including the person you are endorsing and the opportunity you are endorsing them for -- school, job, or promotion.

Introduce Yourself

In additional to identifying the purpose of the letter, you need to introduce yourself to the reader and explain your relationship to the applicant. This should not require more than one or two lines, but you definitely need to include information on how you know the candidate. Examples include:

- The candidate worked for you in the past or is currently your direct report. Mention the company and the titles you both held.

- The candidate is a current or former co-worker. Identify the company you work/worked for, titles, and department/function you both hold.

- The candidate is a current or former student. Explain what you teach in general and what classes the person studied with you.

- The candidate is a friend or associate. This could include members of a team you coach, a member of your youth group or volunteer organization, or a family associate. You will want to explain how you know the candidate and what type of interaction you had/have.

Explaining your relationship to the person you are endorsing is important so the reader can put the information you provide into the proper frame of reference. A direct report accessing their manager will have different things to say than a manager evaluating their employee. Understanding how you know the subject of your letter will help the reader appreciate why you highlight the things you do.

Explain Your Qualifications

During the process of introducing yourself and explaining your relationship with the subject of the letter, you need to qualify yourself to the reader. In other words, convince the reader that your opinion matters and make he or she interested in what you have to say.

As Steve Elcan, the regional sales director at Oracle, explained, *"The most important thing to me is who the letter of recommendation is from. I want to know that the person writing me has some firm ground to recommend this person for the position I am interviewing them for. I care more about what the CEO of an IT company has to say than the CEO of bakery."*

While I have explained that anyone can write a letter of recommendation, as Steve points out, the reader will want to know why what you have to say matters. While this letter is not for promoting yourself, highlighting your qualifications can help enhance your endorsement of the subject of the letter.

Remember the Value of Honesty

After you introduce yourself and explain your qualifications, as you prepare to talk about the candidate, remember the most valuable rule of career hunting: **honesty**.

I prepare a wide-array of career management documents for my clients daily, ranging from resumes and cover letters (the most common) to

thank-you letters, professional biographies, and LinkedIn profiles. In this process, I am told confidential information that I would never include in any of my final products. It is simply not my job to highlight negatives in any way.

Over the course of my career, I have worked with some excellent career coaches – some of whom have contributed to this book – and I believe they could coach their clients to overcome just about any professional setback you could imagine. But in their work – and mine – honestly is vital because anything less can void out offers of employment at any given time.

While I paint my clients in the best possible light, I do not deceive or mislead the individuals reading my work. I do not knowingly include false information or encourage my clients to overstate any aspect of their experience or credentials. If they did not finish college, then that's what is put down. If they have employment gaps, they do not change the dates to make it look like they do not. I strongly recommend you follow the same idea in writing your letter of recommendation.

Promoting the individual you are writing the letter about does not call for exaggeration or falsifying information. The hiring director or admissions committee might never discover your deceit, but if they do, you have made yourself, and the candidate, look bad.

In addition to looking bad if deception is discovered, the job or school candidate might be caught off guard if you put something in your letter that they cannot speak to in an interview. You need to include accurate information that if the person is asked to go into details on, they can do so with ease. Additionally, you need to be able to discuss the information in your letter in additional detail if someone decides to follow up with you. Simply put, **honesty is the best policy**.

Include Achievements & Results

As important as honesty is in a letter of recommendation, even with "truth-in-advertising" laws, companies project themselves in the best possible light. A letter of recommendation should paint someone in a positive light as well, and not focus on drawbacks or negatives or areas in need of improvement, if you mention those ideas at all.

When you talk about an individual's achievements or qualifications, highlighting specific accomplishments can be valuable to bringing weight to your statements. If you feel comfortable talking about specific dollar figures and percentages, please do so. If not, feel free to use general language that still conveys the importance of the work.

If you have written a resume or cover letter for yourself, you likely included achievements in one or both of those documents. For letters of recommendations, you should try to bring to life the accomplishments of the person you are writing the letter for just as you would in your own resume or cover letter. One common strategy for communicating achievements in career documents is **STAR** --**situation**, **task**, **action**, and **result**.

You can translate this strategy for letters of recommendation by thinking of a situation that the person of the letter faced, describing the task and action taken regarding the situation, and then mention the result. While you might often use this strategy to write bullets in a resume or cover letter, you can do it in a story-telling, paragraph format in a letter of recommendation. Consider the following categories you might be able to speak to in a letter of recommendation:

Can the person make money?

Did you witness the subject of the letter generate income, increase sales, or bring in new customers? You can use fundraising activity to demonstrate an ability to make money as well; this includes volunteer work and student activities.

Can the person save money or lower costs?

Did the subject of your letter help reduce costs for your organization? Did you work with this person on a streamlining project that eliminated unnecessary expenditures? Can you talk about their work with vendors or price negotiations?

Does the person introduce improvements or innovation?

Have you worked with this individual to develop new products, processes, or training courses? Are there other creative endeavors you can mention in your letter of recommendation? Both employers and schools like to invest in creative and innovative individuals, so mentioning these skill sets could serve the subject of your letter well. In addition to pure creativity or innovation, you can also talk about improvements to systems or processes that improved the performance or your company. If you can mention specific metrics, that is great; but if not, you can still mention these achievements in vague terms. Just be prepared to discuss the work in greater detail if a hiring manager or admissions coordinator decides to follow up with you.

Did the candidate demonstrate leadership or initiative?

Whether the person you are writing the letter for is seeking a professional position or academic opportunity, the people evaluating his or her candidacy will likely be impressed with demonstrations of leadership skills or initiative. If you can speak of instances where the subject of your letter showcased either leadership or self-motivation should prove beneficial to their candidacy.

Do you award the candidate any honors or recognitions?

If you personally nominated the candidate for an award or special honors that he or she has won, you should make mention of that in your letter. Include information about the award for which you nominated them, why you nominated them, and any other details of the recognition. Also, if you just know of any awards the person received or if you won team recognition together, you can include information about that.

It is important to keep your letter relatively brief so you do not lose the attention of the reader. Therefore, you only need to use one or two examples of these STARs and, in addition to communicating the value of the candidate, he or she should seek to answer one or more of the questions covered in the following section.

Answering Questions the Reader Wants to Know

In a social setting, when you introduce someone to your circle of friends or group of acquaintances, you are expected to help ease that person into a conversation with your friends – not just tell them their name and expect them to impress the new group on their own.

Obviously, with a letter of recommendation, you are expected to talk about the subject of the letter, but it is important to focus on what they can do rather than what they will gain from the company or school you are addressing. The reader of your letter knows what his or her company/school program offers. The reader likely believes that anyone hired by the company or admitted to the school will benefit from the selection. Focusing on those things will do little to distinguish the subject of your letter.

Therefore, you need to put yourself into the mind of the reader and ask yourself what you would want to know about this candidate if you were the decision maker. Some questions might include: What will this person do for me? How does this person align with my organization? Will hiring/admitting this person improve my company/school in the long run?

No matter how long your letter of recommendation is, **the answer to these questions must be clearly stated and easy for the reader to grasp**.

What will this person do for me?

That is the question the hiring manager – and even to some extent admissions director – wants answered as he or she skims your letter of recommendation. What does this person bring to their company or school? How can this person increase their revenue or help their academic program excel? How can the person improve the organization's image or productivity?

To answer this question, you need to know several things about the person you are recommending and the position or school to which they are applying. Now, agreeing to write a letter of recommendation is not a commitment to tons of research. Therefore, the person who asks you to write the letter should provide you with a job description or information about their academic program. If they do not automatically provide this information, ask them for it and explain how the letter will be incomplete or lacking without it.

Once you have an opportunity to examine the job listing or description of the academic program to which the person is applying, you can begin identifying things you know about the subject of the letter that meets the company's/school's needs. This is how your letter will begin to take shape.

One key indicator of a person's future success are examples of achievements from their past. Sometimes an achievement might easily demonstrate a person's skills or abilities. Other times, you might need to do a bit of storytelling to properly convey the message to the reader. Please see below for examples of both approaches.

Examples of Achievements:

"When I was working with Bill at Company Name, he negotiated and secured a $500K+ contract with one vendor for due diligence nationwide that created more than $100K in cost savings."

"At Company Name, I was impressed with Cathy's success in launching a new software application that surpassed sales and revenue targets by 30% within the first six months of release."

Examples of Stories:

"Victor and I have been active members of our Chamber of Commerce for years. I have seen him work tirelessly to bring in new businesses and foster a sense of community pride in our city. Even though his work as an engineer is highly technical, I have no

doubt he will provide solid leadership as he seeks to transition into management roles."

"As Ashley's piano and guitar instructor, it has been my pleasure to guide her through the process of mastering two instruments. I can attest to her diligence and passion in the pursuit of her musical instruments. From what I know of her academic achievements, I believe this pursuit of excellence is evident in all she does and will translate to your program as well."

"I had the privilege of training Jenna before leaving my position at Company Name for my current role. During that time Jenna demonstrated the ability to learn quickly and adapt to diverse expectations. Besides producing career packages, she also contributed to academic curriculum and company marketing material. Jenna showed both drive and willingness to learn from others, a key attributes in a new employee."

Will this person fit into my organization?

Most companies and academic institutions will dedicate a portion of their websites to communicating their vision, core values, and other pertinent information. If you can easily search out this information about the company or school you are addressing in your letter of recommendation, you might find some key words you can include when describing the subject of your letter.

If the company has a strong dedication to community involvement, talk about the person's work with Habitat for Humanity. If the school has demonstrated a commitment to research and development, speak about the person's natural curiosity and problem solving skills.

Addressing this part of the reader's question might not even require specific achievements or storytelling; it might just require you to use some of the company's or school's same terminology throughout your letter.

Examples:

*"When I left IT-R-Us to found my current company with a long-time friend, I tried to persuade Janice into coming with me. Unfortunately for me, Janice feels more at home in a larger corporation. **I believe her career aspirations align very well with your organization's needs.** Since she is fluent in Spanish and French, I know she is particularly interested in **leveraging her foreign language skills in your overseas operations.**"*

*"Since our time working together, Ayla earned an MBA and held two management positions. Even when she was working for me, I could see she had a talent for managing and training staff. I believe the combination of her sales and leadership talent will make her a fine additional to your sales organization. **Additionally, she has a rich network in the state of Florida having spent her childhood there and attended the University of Florida for her MBA.**"*

*"**I highly recommend Ayla for your Sales Director role in Florida.** I believe she will make an immediate impact on your top-lines and infuse a positive energy into your sales team. If I can be of any additional assistance as you evaluate her candidacy, please let me know. Thank you for your time."*

*"**As an alumnus of your school, I know that Keith will fit in well to the Graduate Program.** He brings a great passion for writing, photography, and layout to his work, and I'm sure that will lead to several positive contributions to your programs. I intend to use Keith on a stringer basis as often as I can, but I have no doubt he will effectively immerse himself into your print products and on-line news offerings in no time."*

Will this person benefit my organization in the long run?

When a resource is scarce, competition for the resource is fierce. Both jobs and academic slots are a highly sought after resource right now. Your letter of recommendation should help the recipient position himself/herself ahead of their competition. To do so, you need to help communicate to the reader why the subject of the letter is worth their investment over another applicant.

Companies and schools are no longer looking only for people who will excel in the classroom or perform their job duties in an exceptional manner. They are also looking for a long-term return on investment. Does this mean the person needs to work for that organization for ten years or remain a part of the university system upon graduation? No. But it does mean that you should highlight how the subject of the letter can enhance the company or school's reputation or brand in the future.

This might not always be something you can speak to in your letter and it is all right if you do not include something along these lines. However, when addressing a school admissions director, if you can state your belief that the candidate will be an excellent student and a successful business person upon graduation, it reinforces the idea that this person will be a positive reflection on the school.

When addressing a hiring manager, if you can say that you believe the applicant will make a fine sales manager and that they show promise that would facilitate advancement into territory management, you can communicate to the reader that this person is someone they can mentor for the future.

Provide a Means of Follow Up

One final note regarding the content strategy: it is important to make sure the reader knows he/she can contact you if he/she has any additional questions about the candidate. Whether or not he/she calls you is not the important thing – it is vital that you communicate that you are more than happy to talk about the candidate further. The fact that you are will to speak about the subject of the letter in greater detail tells the reader you are fully committed to endorsing that person. Be sure to include a valid phone number and email address in the header of the letter, closing paragraph, or both.

PART TWO

*T*he second section of the book details different types of letters of recommendation; these include both professional and academic letters of recommendation as well as networking introductions and performance evaluations.

This section includes the following elements of our 10-step checklist

- Identify the letter's audience and tailoring it for the recipient.
- Define the candidate's strengths and ask if there is anything they want you to highlight.
- Write the draft of your letter and editing it for final content.

The importance of reviewing these different types of letters of recommendation is that the focus of your letter will vary depending on your audience and your relationship to the reader. This section will provide you with strategies for all of those circumstances.

Chapter 6

The Professional Letter of Recommendation, Part 1

he professional letter of recommendation can be written by any professional and for any professional. The relationship you have with the subject of the letter will impact the skills, achievements, and characteristics you can address in your letter which will be explored in greater detail in the next chapter. It is important to remember that if you cannot answer at least some of the questions the hiring manager wants to learn about the candidate, your letter of recommendation may fall on deaf ears.

Content that Matters

When you are writing a letter of recommendation for someone's professional pursuits, you know intuitively that you need to speak about their professional abilities in some way. Unless the hiring manager is looking to hire a gardener, they do not want to hear about someone's gardening hobby. It might be acceptable to talk about a person's community service or even academic achievements, depending on their experience level, but only if you can use those topics to communicate business skills or key character traits.

If you are a hiring manager, it might be easy to put yourself in the reader's shoes and identify what you would want to know about the candidate. Thinking of what questions you would like answered is a good place to start. However, if you lack experience in interviewing or recruiting or you do not know on what to focus your letter, consider the following advice from career coaches and human resource managers.

Paula Rue, the human resources director at Economic Recovery Group, LLC said, *"Although this is a professional document – and it is an important piece to the person's professional portfolio – it needs to be personal. The letter should mention **specific achievements about the person** and it should mention **something personal about the person.** Something that says more about their personality than their skill set."* Paula recommends that you consider the following questions when planning your letter:

- Did he/she save the company money?
- Did he/she develop something for the company?
- Did he/she improve performance or a process?
- What do you remember most about this person?
- Are they always on time?
- Are they known by the majority of the staff as a person that they can turn to when they need help?
- Do they stand out as a key player?
- Do they have great interpersonal skills?
- Are the flexible?
- Do they adapt to change easily?

According to Valerie El-Jamil, *Executive, Career, & Transition Coach,* you will want to speak to a person's **behavior traits, your history with the candidate,** and **their ability to perform**. Some of the questions she recommends you answer include:

- How does this person lead/manage?
- How does this person work with others or build collaboration?
- In what type of corporate culture does this person perform best?
- How well does this person do their job?
- What type of work ethic does this person have?
- How well does the candidate perform under pressure?
- Would you hire the candidate yourself?

Fred Coon, author of *Ready Aim Hired* and CEO of Stewart, Cooper, & Coon, counsels clients that each letter should contain one or two short stories with key words that highlight core competencies and key accomplishments. The meat of the story should be no more than five lines, one to two paragraphs, and the writer should describe a project and provide a frame of reference that adds a personal flare to the letter.

Reviewing a person's resume or performance evaluations prior to writing the letter of recommendation will help you answer many of these questions. In fact, Paula Rue said, *"As a human resources director, the first thing I do (when writing a letter of recommendation) is pull all their performance reviews. If your company has a performance review process in place, it makes writing a letter of recommendation – plug and play!"*

However, do not be tempted to borrow a highlight from the person's resume with which you are unfamiliar. According to El-Jamil, it is not a good idea to write a letter that cannot be backed up with a phone conference. There is a possibility that the person you are writing the letter to will want to ask you additional questions. You only want to include items in your letter that you can speak to comfortably and in detail in a later conversion.

Experience Matters

A hiring manager will not expect an entry-level professional's resume to look the same as an executive's, nor will they expect the things covered in a letter of recommendation to be similar. Do not attempt to make an entry-level professional look like a person with five or ten years of solid work experience. Instead, leverage their academic training and non-career experience to promote skills the hiring manager will want to see. In contrast, do not focus on an executive's education, but rather their experience and accomplishments.

Depending on when your letter of recommendation is requested, you could be framing the candidate in the hiring manager's mind before the first interview or helping distinguish the candidate from a group of two or three final contestants. It is important that you present the candidate in a light that is consistent with both experience and the position he or she is seeking.

Therefore, the focus of your content must be adjusted based on the experience the person you are writing about possesses. This is another reason why taking a look at their resume prior to writing your letter could be of use. You might know a great deal about the person now, but a brief view of their professional history could be helpful in deciding the tone and emphasis your letter should take.

Recommendations for an Entry-Level Professional

No matter how you know the entry-level professional, writing their letter of recommendation will likely require reaching beyond their professional experience and drawing connections between non-work experience and skills the reader wants to see. You can draw these connections from the person's academic work, community service, academic/school achievements, or work study/part-time employment. In each case, the key is to review the job description for things the hiring manager wants to know about the candidate and tie that to a skill you witnessed the person demonstrate. A few examples follow for each situation mentioned above.

Academic Work

In this instance, you are most likely the subject's professor, counselor, or have some other academic relationship to the recipient of your letter. In this case, you can certainly speak about coursework and masterly of subject matter, but you can also go into how the person performed on academic projects or in classroom activities such as speeches or small group discussions.

Example:

"William was an excellent student and always delivered his work on time and to the highest quality standards. But he did more than just master the course material; he was a constant leader in group discussions and helped fellow classmates understand concepts they missed during lectures. A couple of weeks into the semester, he took the initiative to organize student-lead study sessions that greatly benefited those who participated.

My opinion of William is that his is more than just an excellent student; he is also a natural organizer and team leader. This is backed up by his position as captain of a student intramural basketball league and membership chair of his fraternity. As he progresses in his job duties, I have no doubt that he will find opportunities to help his team members improve in their performance while delivering at peak levels himself."

"Ashley is a naturally gifted speaker and she always appeared at ease when addressing her classmates for presentations. She would communicate the facts of her presentations with in-depth knowledge

and answer questions from her classmates with confidence. When called upon to participate in classroom discussions, she provided interesting insight to the material and could draw upon her knowledge of news and current events to deepen the discussions.

Ashley did well in my class, but I saw much more in her than a mastery of my subject material. She demonstrated a passion for the subject area and I have been informed by her other professor that she brought the same energy to their classrooms as well. I believe she will continue to pursue education and training in this area and should prove valuable to you as she progresses in expertise and ability."

Community Service

You do not have to be the president of an organization or committee chair to recommend someone you work with in a community service organization or group. If you have worked closely with the person on several completed projects or on-going tasks, you have observed skill sets that you can address in your letter of recommendation.

Example:

"Janice and I handled the marketing and organization of our group's last charity walk where the proceeds of the fundraising went to a local children's hospital. Janice's youth and exuberance made long days on the project go by easier, but it was her perseverance in recruiting participants and support personnel that really made the walk a success.

Janice also presented several creative ideas for marketing the event, including the use of social media outlets such as Facebook and Twitter. She even tweeted several comments while she participated in the walk herself! She proved invaluable to our fundraising efforts which resulted in double the amount we raised last year without her.

> *I know she is pursuing a sales position, which she is exceptionally qualified for, but I believe she has an amazing future in team leadership and motivation as well. I highly recommend that you hire her and mentor her for future positions of responsibility in your company."*

School Achievements

Whether winning a scholarship or earning a starting spot on the school's basketball team, a school achievement can convey several skills that hiring managers want to see in their candidates. You can talk about a person's school achievements and tie in into their academic work if you are a professor, resident director, or organization sponsor. This should allow you to give a more complete assessment of the candidate beyond your direct involvement with the subject of your letter while still staying within the body of experience the reader will expect you to cover.

Example:

> *"As Matthew's speech and English literature instructor, I had the privilege of witnessing his commitment to coursework firsthand. He was an inquisitive learner who frequently went above and beyond in his assignments. His speech work was particularly exceptional as he presented information effectively and impactful.*
>
> *However, the thing that impressed me the most was how Matthew did so well my courses while maintaining his basketball scholarship. The demands on his time between his courses and athletics left little time for socializing I am sure, but he continued to excel at both. I believe this demonstrates a talent for time and resource management that will prove valuable in his professional pursuits."*
>
> *"My experience with John was as the sponsor of the College of Journalism's faculty director for the student government. John served as the secretary and later president of the organization.*

During his tenure, he effectively represented the school to the larger university governing body while shaping policies that positive impacted the school's student body.

During this time, I know John maintained a grade level that qualified him to graduate with honors. I have spoken to several of my colleagues in the College of Journalism and they all speak highly of his dedication in the classroom and work product."

Part-Time Employment

The manager of a retail operation, restaurant, or other business where a student has worked part-time can be an impactful reference for an entry-level professional. You might not know much about the student's academics and the person might be pursuing a career completed unrelated to the work they did for you, but that is no reason you cannot write them a recommendation. You are a great source to speak on the subject's work ethic and professionalism.

Example:

"Eric worked for me at Retail Company between 15 and 20 hours a week while maintaining a full load in school. While we had to accommodate his school schedule, he gave advanced noticed when he needed time off and always met his work commitments.

Eric displayed excellent professionalism and performed all assigned tasks, from customer service to backroom stocking, without complaint. He was always one of the first employees to learn about new products and present them to our customers.

I believe his ability to manage his coursework while performing his work duties for me demonstrates his ability to multitask and plan his schedule well. You will find he is an excellent employee who learns fast and is highly reliable."

Recommendations for a Mid-Level Professional

If a person has several years of experience, you will not need to speak much about his/her academic experience – if at all. You can mention certifications, licenses, or relevant training they have completed recently, but otherwise, you can focus strongly on professional accomplishments.

Other areas you can cover are community service work or professional organizations where you have interacted with the subject of your letter. In these instances, you still need to focus on demonstrating professional skills. If the person is applying for a position similar to the one they are currently in, you should be able to just focus on their qualifications for the role. On the other hand, if the person is seeking advancement, you might need to address signs of potential in your letter.

Example:

"Having worked with David on the company's most recent SAP implementation, I can attest to his planning and management skills. He organized the implementation effort in just a couple of weeks and had it implemented – without downtime – in all of our offices in less than a month. He completed the project in time for my team to utilize the program in our busiest season. I was also impressed with how well he trained my team and supported them in using the program until everyone felt completely confident."

"One of the many areas in which Emily excels is her ability to effectively manage vendor relationships. For over a year now, in addition to her other duties, she has handled the selection of office suppliers and the purchasing of all of communications/office products and services. As a result of her management, we have saved 15 percent of our budget compared to the last year.

It is my understanding that position she is seeking will involve this responsibility on a much greater level. To support her interest in this position, she has recently completed budgeting and vendor management training sessions internally. Based on my experience, I believe Emily will perform exceptionally in this capacity."

Recommendations for an Executive

No matter the industry, executive-level leadership usually means the person has control over a team and a budget of some size and typically the ability to impact the company's bottom-line. A letter of recommendation for an executive should touch on at least one of these points. If your interaction with the executive is outside of a professional venue, you should at least be able to speak to their leadership capabilities. If you do not know the details of your company's revenue or profit performance, you should still be able to speak to improvements you have witnessed in efficiency, customer satisfaction, quality, or employee engagement.

Example:

"Sam is an exceptional operations leader, the best I have ever worked for in fact. He is continuously on the floor of our operation making sure adequate safety protocols are in place and that employees feel valued. The corporate culture that has evolved as a result is one where I hardly have to concern myself with employee turnover or low-quality work.

Sam also prioritizes our customers. He holds regularly scheduled meetings with his managers and client representatives to ensure open communications and that we completely understand the customers' needs. This has proven helpful in ensuring the final product we deliver completely adheres to client expectations and contract specifications."

"Beth has positively impacted our revenue production from within six months of taking on the Executive Sales role. Now that we are growing and reorganizing, she wants to take on greater responsibilities and I believe we would only benefit by offering her that opportunity."

"As a Certified Six Sigma Black Belt, Helen has identified several areas for improvement and planned six sigma projects that have greatly

enhanced our efficiency and profitability. She mentors her project managers on our targeted end results to help them understand the impact of the projects they are leading. This has resulted in successful implementation of new technologies, methods, and process improvements that lowered costs 20 percent over two years."

Avoid Templates

If you have gotten this far in the book, you might be thinking it would be much easier just to look up a template online; after all, they have templates for everything online, right? As a resume writer, I am predisposed to dislike templates. I see client resumes come across my desk that are t based on some popular resume template the person found online but are poorly written and badly formatted. The best resumes are customized in both content and format to meet the individual's specific career needs. The same is true for letters of recommendation.

"When writing a letter of recommendation for an employee past or present the tone and length of the letter depend on the quality of their employment. Bottom-line: if they were a great employee their letter is customized, but if they were just okay, the letter becomes a bit more robotic," says HR Manager Paula Rue.

The subtext of Paula's quote is clear. If you produce a letter of recommendation that looks like it came from a template, the letter will fail to impress the reader. If you think about it, this really does make sense. If the person you are writing the letter for did not impress you enough for you to spend 30 minutes writing a letter from scratch, why would that person impress the reader?

In addition to emphasizing the need to customize your letter of recommendation, you should avoid "borrowing" too much from samples as well.

"There are a lot of samples online (and in this book) that you can reference, but you should avoid pulling language from them too closely. I have heard of people getting called on the carpet for their letters of recommendation sounding too much like a sample posted online.

If you are concerned about writing a good letter of recommendation for each person who asks you for one, you can create your own personal template. You will need to edit for each individual that asks you for a letter, but you can setup your letterhead, information about who you are and the company you work for, and any other information that is frequently used in each letter you write. This will not save you much time, but it could give you a little shortcut for the letter writing process," said Executive Career Coach Valerie El-Jamil.

Note to Applicants

If you are concerned about the person you are asking to write the letter not having time, you can consider the advice of Fred Coon, author of *Ready Aim Hired* and CEO of Stewart, Cooper, & Coon on planning winning content for letters of recommendations.

Coon advises his clients to assemble six to nine letters of recommendations that they can leave behind after an interview. He says each letter should tell a story of what they can do. Working together, the letters should allow the reader to get a feeling that the person can actually DO something.

Coon tells his clients to write the letters themselves and call their references and say, "I know you are busy and I am going to structure the body of the letter for you. Please feel free to add a personal note about me to the framework that I send you." Coon says that just as your resume is one tool in the job search arsenal, the letter of recommendation is another important tool, and you should make sure your letters are strong and ready for use as you interview for new positions.

Chapter 7

The Professional Letter of Recommendation, Part 2

As mentioned before, the relationship between letter writer and recipient can strongly impact the content covered in the letter of recommendation. Additionally, the situation for which the letter is being written may impact the material you want to cover as well. Examples include writing a letter for a manager or direct report, writing a letter for an open position within your company, or writing a letter for a job opening at a different company. This chapter will explore these differences and how you can write a solid letter under any circumstance.

The Business Relationship

Your business relationship with your co-workers, managers, and direct reports are all valuable commodities, and you certainly do not want to put them at risk by agreeing to write a letter of recommendation and then writing a poor one. Your letter of recommendation is an investment in that relationship much more so than it is a favor. Therefore, take the time to make a sound investment.

To begin the brainstorming process for the letter of recommendation, consider your relationship with the subject of the letter. Does this person work for you? Do you work for them? Are you equals, team members, or business associates? Since you will identify your relationship with the subject of the letter early on, it is important to frame your endorsement in that light.

Do not speak to things of which you should have no knowledge, but keep you focus on things you can testify to first hand. While you can review the person's resume for a reference point, do not talk about details you are not familiar with personally. Taking this approach to writing your recommendation will strengthen the validity of your letter and the impact it will make on the reader.

Writing a Letter for a Coworker

If you have been asked by a coworker or business associate to write a letter of recommendation, you are going to be speaking about work you have collaborated on or business you have done together. Characteristics or skills you might be addressing could include:

- Teamwork
- Communications
- Collaboration/Problem Solving
- Negotiations
- Support (Technical or Business)
- Operations
- Process Improvements
- Collaborative Sales
- Customer Relations/Service
- Project Management/Implementation
- Strategic/Planning

If you work on the same team, performing similar job duties, you will be able to describe work you have done together, situations where the individual helped you complete or improve you work, positive comments you have heard clients give the subject of your letter, and significant team achievements, honors, and awards.

Remember you do not want to speak on achievements or areas of expertise with which you are not familiar. Of course the fuller picture you can provide the reader in your letter, the stronger impression you will leave, but false praise that you cannot back up with specific examples will not benefit the subject of your letter. If you know the person in a social setting or you have worked on committees, charities, or fundraising events together, then you can speak to related issues.

If you have witnessed the subject of your letter's interaction with clients, co-workers, and/or family, you can talk about some personality traits if you feel it will be helpful to his/her application. However, professional contacts should focus on promoting characteristics and skills you have experience in professional settings.

Writing a Letter for a Direct Report

As a manager writing a letter of recommendation for a direct report, you will be able to speak to how well the subject of the letter performs his/her job, in what areas he/she excels, and how the person relates to others in a work environment.

If you feel the person has potential for leadership or management development, you should point this out in your letter of recommendation. However, if you bring this up, you should be prepared to support it with facts of some sort. Make sure you reference their performance evaluations if you still have access to them. This will allow you to review how you evaluated their job performance and what areas you have previously identified for improvement.

If you can identify a pattern of improvement when it comes to performance achievements and an effort to continuously improve one's skills and capabilities, be sure to point these things out in your letter of recommendation.

Writing a Letter for a Manager

If your manager has come to you and asked you to write them a letter of recommendation, this mean he/she needs a direct reports evaluation of their leadership capabilities. In these instances, discuss the subject's leadership approach, the success the team enjoyed underneath his/her leadership, and the type of environment this person sought to create for teams and clients.

The Job Opening

Just like the business relationship makes a difference in the content you contain in the letter, whether you are writing the letter of recommendation for an internal opening or a position at another company makes a difference as well. This section examines each situation in detail.

Writing for a Coworker applying to an Internal Opening

When you are writing a letter for a coworker or business associate for an internal opening, you are putting your reputation at risk. It does not matter if you are recommending someone from outside of your company for the new hire or someone with whom you work, you will hear from the hiring manager how your recommended recruit is doing whether or not that person works out.

It is vital that you protect yourself for potential lawsuits by not detailing out negatives or writing anything in your letter of recommendation that could keep the person from earning the new job. It is also important that you only agree to write the letter of recommendation if you are confident the person will work out in the role for which you are endorsing them.

In this setting, the letter of recommendation might not need to be as formal as in other settings, but you need to check company policy on delivery and make sure you adhere to it. You should still make sure you review the details of the job listing to make sure you have selected key words and phrases that will catch the reader's attention.

<u>Example</u>

I am writing you on behalf of Tonya Jones to recommend her as Lead Pharmacist at our new location in Atlanta, Georgia. Tonya and I have served as the two main Pharmacists in our Ocala, Florida, location for the past five years. She is now looking to relocate as a result of her husband's career and I strongly believe we should work to keep her in-house. Additionally, a new store would benefit immensely from Tonya's knowledge and expertise.

Tonya displays a high level of customer service to our diverse customer-base. She is very familiar with the medicines prescribed to senior patients as we have a large-retirement community nearby. She is also highly skilled at addressing questions for parents of school aged children, and regularly volunteers to administer required immunizations to local students.

Tonya manages our inventory levels, ensuring we were well stocked on all needed medications and supplies. Together we regularly monitored inventory and accounted for any loss we encountered. I have been told our stockroom is one of the best maintained in the company, with zero infractions for controlled substances.

You will find Tonya friendly and willing to help patients get needed medicines even when issues arose with their insurance providers and/or doctor's offices. Our Rx numbers have actually increased significantly over the last five years, and I believe that is based in part on how much our customers like Tonya.

I encourage you to consider her for the new store and will be happy to answer any questions you might have in this regards. Please feel free to contact me at the above phone number or email. Thank you for your time.

Writing for a Coworker applying to Another Company

If you are recommending a coworker of yours for a position in another company, you likely have less concern for reprisal if it does not work out between the new company and the new employee (your contact), but a negative – or less than stellar – review could have potentially negative outcomes for you and the subject of the letter.

When writing this letter you will want to make sure you have a solid understanding of the job opening and then communicate facts you know about the employee and how the candidate's skills align well with the new company.

<u>Example written by a Current Coworker</u>

Jason Thomas asked me to contact you on his behalf for the role of Technician Team Leader and I am very pleased to do so. Jason has been working in the areas of wireless, telecom, and networks for more than ten years (five of which we worked for the same company). He is very knowledgeable in building infrastructure and networks, maintaining network/server performance, and upgrading technology tools as needed.

I've worked with Jason on numerous projects over the last five years, including a transition to Cisco routers, switchers, and servers. We also completed an infrastructure revamp that improved performance 25 percent. Jason regularly commits to providing 24/7 technical support to help some of our employees with more family obligations. At this point, Jason is simply looking for roles with greater scope and accountability than we can provide, but I strong endorse him for your company.

When it comes to credentials, I know Jason has several Cisco and tool certifications. He is also highly adept at Agile and SDLC methodologies. Jason is not just knowledgeable on technical tools and applications, but also affective at translating that expertise in project oversight for major clients. Additionally, he offers some success in managing team members and budgets.

I strongly endorse Jason's application for you technical team and believe you will benefit from his presence. I appreciate the time you have taken to read this letter. If you have any questions, please just contact me at the phone or email address above.

Example written by a Former Coworker

I am pleased to write to you on behalf of Michael R. Andrews, recommending him for your open position of Operations Manager. I worked with Michael and XYZ Corporation for five years and can attest to his ability to effectively run a production floor in a manufacturing environment. My job was to oversee the safety and environmental compliance functions of our operation, and Michael fully supported my efforts.

While I worked to achieve and maintain ISO certifications, Michael organized training sessions to ensure our policies and procedures were fully understood and adhered all production floor workers in a 24/7 environment. Michael placed a strong emphasis on making sure production equipment was well maintained, and I often worked with him to decide when machines and tools needed to refurbished or replaced.

Despite adoption of stricter regulations, Michael still increased his production numbers and quality ratings during his time at XYZ Corporation. As a manager, Michael is well-respected and shows his employees that he gives as much as he demands. He takes an active approach to mentoring his assistance managers and other staff members.

I believe Michael will make an immediate, positive difference in your organization, and I highly endorse his application. If I can answer any additional questions about Michael's work, please feel free to call me on my cell at 555-555-5555 or email me on my personal account at beckyr@email.com. Thank you for your time.

Writing for a Direct Report applying for an Internal Opening

When writing a letter of recommendation for a direct report to an internal opening, you are likely addressing a peer and the letter should be written as such. While often in a letter of recommendation, you only know the subject of the letter; when you do know the reader, the letter should reflect that in tone.

In this circumstance, when addressing the reader, you can bring up specific projects or assignments which the reader will be familiar with and describe the work the subject of your letter performed during this time. You are also free to use acronyms or company lingo you know the reader of the letter will understand.

In this form of letter writing, you should address the candidate's capabilities and bring up several examples of company contributions the individual has completed. It could even be relevant to list these in a bulleted format.

Paragraph Example

I am writing to you to recommend John for the position in your department of Client Services Manager. John has worked for me for two years as an Account Executive as has proven highly productive in this role. I believe he will prove to be an asset as a manager in your department and completely endorse him for the position.

I find John to be hard-working, energetic, and full of initiative. Upon being hired, John was assigned stable, but non-growth accounts as a learning tool until he became more familiar with our products and services. Within six months, John had achieved a 10 percent increase in account spending with three clients that had not changed their business with us in five years! As a result, I assigned John to a few client presentations, and he landed them all.

Despite his entire account listings being made up of old accounts or newly on-boarded clients, John is one of the highest revenue producers on my team. I believe his key to success is his passion for our products and exceptional talent for customer service. This is why I so strongly recommend him for your open role. I know if he can train a team to do what he does, we will note a significant decrease in client complaints and attrition.

If I can be of any additional assistance in your evaluations process, please let me know. My direct line is 555-555-5555 or you can reach me by email at loriwilliams@email.com. Of course feel free to stop by my office to go over any questions you might have any time.

Bulleted Example

Charles Williams has asked me to contact you on his behalf to recommend his application for your payroll specialist. Charles has been part of our accounting department since 2011, working on a wide-range of financial management responsibilities and achievements. Consider these examples of his work:

- *Expertly processes payroll for 150 salary, full-time, and part-time employees while handling billing for major corporate clients.*

- *Partners with co-worker to handling hundreds of small- to mid-level clients.*

- *Reduced aged receivables 30 percent over the past year and dramatically improved the company's cash flow as a result.*

I was notably impressed when Charles represented our department for IT's implementation of new financial management/accounting software. He ensured they incorporated everything we needed into the new system and that there was no interruption to payroll or billing.

On a personal level, Charles organized our company's Toys-4-Tots efforts and encouraged us all to sponsor his charity efforts for Walk for a Cure last year.

I believe he will prove himself an instant asset due to his detailed, accurate work as well as his efforts to create a positive work environment. I appreciate the time you have taken to read this letter. If I can provide any additional information to help you review Charles's candidacy, please feel free to call me at 555-555-5555 or email me at probinson@emailaddress.com.

Writing for a Direct Report applying to a position at Another Company

Whereas the previous category might be more casual in nature, this situation would demand a more formal approach to letters of recommendation. You will want to make sure your letter follows a clean business format like the ones we provide in the last few sections of the book. You will also want to make sure your font options have proven fruitful in formal business meetings/settings.

Example

Jacob Smith has asked me to write to you recommending his work as a Project Manager for my company, Construction Services, Inc. It is my pleasure to give him the highest recommendation for his project management, client relations, and budgetary skills.

Jacob has been an asset in planning and executing high value government and commercial contracts. His experience in the US Army's Core of engineers gives him an edge in working with military personnel, and he quickly became my go-to-guy for defense contracts in the southeastern United States.

One of Jacob's greatest strengths is his ability to bring contractors, subcontractors, city/state agency representatives, and other stakeholders together in an efficient effort to carry out a client's needs. He always delivered his projects on-time and typically under budget. But I have to say the skill that impressed me the most was his ability to deal with clients that micromanaged or frequently requested changes in the construction plan. He was always able to deliver high levels of service, no matter how extreme the client pressure got.

Over the last seven years, Jacob has enjoyed traveling for work and was one of the best on-site managers I could have asked for. Now that he and his wife are expecting their second child and they want to live closer to her ailing parents, Jacob has decided to look outside my organization for work so that he can settle in Dallas and focus his time in the Dallas/Fort Worth area.

While my team will miss Jacob, I can assure you that my loss would be your gain, and he will quickly prove to be a valuable member of your team. If I can be of any additional assistance as you consider Jacob's candidacy, please feel free to contact me at the phone or email address listed above.

Writing for a Manager applying to an Internal Opening

If you have been called upon by a manager to write a letter of recommendation while they are working on advancing through their career paths, you want to make sure you convey a solid endorsement of their skill levels and long-term goals or potential.

When writing a recommendation for a manager, you will want to focus on their leadership skills, strategic planning, training and development, ability to communicate goals to their team members, and change management. These are all skills you can attest to on a personal level.

Example

William Patrick Jones has asked me to write to you, recommending his work as a Warehouse and Logistics Manager. I believe he will prove a good fit to your open position and I highly endorse him for the role. William and I have worked together in a supply chain function for the last three years. I admire his tenacious efforts to drive safety, environmental, and regulatory compliance while trying to find the best shipping routes for our company and clients.

Our team has been consistently tapped to handle increases in productions and customer demand, and we have answered this challenge with cost-effective, on-time shipping over land, air, and sea. William has introduced key new processes and tools so that we can achieve our shipping objectives without having to hire new employees or increase costs.

William is interested in the Warehouse & Logistics Manager position because it is a promotion from our current function and I believe he will enjoy the challenge of handling higher volume and revenue responsibility. Additionally, I know William enjoys leading training seminars and sessions to keep employees up-to-date on changes in technology and methodologies, and I believe you will find that beneficial.

William is energetic, hard-working, and fully trained on OSHA-Hazmat requirements. I believe he will make an immediate and lasting impact on the warehouse and logistics functions of the company and encourage you to fully consider his application. I appreciate the time you have take to read this letter. If I can be of any additional assistance, please contact me at the phone number or email address listed above.

Writing for a Manager applying to Another Company

When writing a letter of recommendation for a manager who is now seeking employment elsewhere, you can incorporate the previous suggestions while also communicating to the reader why the employee is looking to switch companies. If the subject of the letter is particularly excited about the new work, feel free to communicate that. Also talk about how this person's leadership has proven so valuable in the past and you are confident this trend will continue.

Example

I am writing to recommend Mr. David West for the opening of Sales Executive, Southeast Region. David has been my managing director for the past seven years, and he has lead our team through periods of significant growth, in revenue and clientele.

David planned and directed multiple sales initiatives, product launches, and openings of new retail locations over that same period of time. I admire his ability to blend creativity with practical business execution of these projects. He is well in tune with customer wants and needs and shapes our sales efforts accordingly.

At the same time, David empowers our sales team to achieve individual growth and success. He sets very aggressive sales targets, but he also takes a hands-on approach to making sure we have all the tools we need to obtain those goals. Since he makes it a point to raise the bar every year, I am often surprised when I make quota, but under David's leadership, I have never missed one.

David's desire to leave our organization is mixed at best, but there is little room for him to continue to progress in his career in our current setup. I know he has a strong passion for your product line, and I believe you will find him a top contributor to both sales and new product development/marketing. If I can answer any additional questions for you, please just contact me at the phone number or email listed above.

Your business relationship
with your co-workers,
managers, and direct reports
are all valuable commodities,
and you certainly do not want
to put them at risk by agreeing to
write a letter of recommendation
and then writing a poor one.

The Academic Letter of Recommendation

The academic letter of recommendation is a diverse category that spans from undergraduate college admissions to graduate school, law school, or medical school. The complexity of evaluations and hurdles the student must overcome vary in difficulty as well. In a highly competitive market for admissions into top schools, and even second tier schools, letters of recommendation can make a strong impact on acceptance or rejection.

In this section, the different types of opportunities that could call for an academic-minded letter of recommendation are examined as well as what the readers of these letters might be looking for in each situation. Also included are some sample letter "bodies" to illustrate key points. Complete examples of academic letters of recommendation can be found in part three of this book.

Undergraduate Programs

An undergraduate applicant might request a letter of recommendation from a high school teacher, a school principal, community leaders, volunteer coordinators, part-time employers, coaches, or clergy. These letters can include information on how the individual did as a student, on a job, as part of a team, or as a member of a volunteer organization. Any time you can touch on more than one area and talk about how the applicant balanced academics, work, and other pursuits well should prove impressive to admissions boards looking for well-rounded individuals.

Any time you can touch on more than one area and talk about how the applicant balanced academics, work, and other pursuits well should prove impressive to admissions boards looking for well-rounded individuals.

Example written by an Employer

Brandon Ericson asked me to write to you regarding his application for admission to your school. I am pleased to recommend him, and I believe you will find him a hard-working, attentive, and ambitious student.

Brandon started working for me part-time during the summer between his junior and senior year of high school and has progressed well during his employment. He has mastered elements of inventory management, merchandising, sales, and customer service over the last year-and-a-half. All of these are standard for working in retail, but Brandon performs at an above average level in each category.

I have managed Brandon's hours around his school schedule and athletic pursuits, and as far as I know, his work has never come into conflict with his academics or sports efforts. Last year Brandon showed incredible initiative and suggested that we purchase ad space in his school's football program. Several customers have come in to our store saying they heard about us through that program, and I decided to purchase more ad space this year as a result.

From everything I know about Brandon, I believe he will prove a solid investment if you admit him to your school. His drive to succeed will lead him to pursue a degree with a strong passion and represent your school well as a future alumnus. If I can answer any additional questions regarding Brandon, please contact me at 555-555-5555 or jameslrobertson@emailaddress.com.

Example written by a Teacher

Farah Fueller has asked me to endorse her application for admission in the University of State and I am pleased to do so. It has been my privilege to have Farah as a student for Biology Honors her sophomore year and now as part of my senior year anatomy class. I have also gotten to know a great deal about Farah as one of the sponsor of our school's National Honor Association (NHA).

As a student, Farah displays a strong curiosity in the sciences and laboratory work. She earned top marks in both the classes I instructed and in all other science courses offered by our department. Farah is a leader in lab experiments and usually helps other students if they are having a difficult time in their lab work.

She is on track to graduate among the top of class, but she has excelled in much more than academics. As a member of the NHA, Farah participated in several fundraising and charity events as well as academic contests. She also participated in our club's tutoring efforts with local elementary students.

Farah effectively balances her academic workload with a steady participation in school sports. It is my understanding that she ran track and lettered on our school's girls' basketball team. It is commendable that she was able to excel in these sports while pursuing the most rigorous academic program our school has to offer, including dual-enrollment courses at the local community college.

I find Farah well deserving of an education at a quality university such as yours, and I believe she will prove a solid member of your student body and future alumni association. I appreciate the time you have spent reading this letter. If I can answer any more questions about Farah, please feel free to call me at 555-555-5555 or email me at my school address: jcollins-wright@highschool.com.

Graduate Schools

A graduate school candidate might be looking for admissions immediately after completing their four-year degree or he or she could be a professional looking to expand their knowledge/capabilities. Therefore, they might request a letter of recommendation of academics or professionals. It is key that the person who writes this letter has direct knowledge of the work and the character of this applicant.

You do not need to attempt to write a letter for someone who you knew several years ago and your familiarity with their work has significantly decreased. Just because someone is applying to a school program does not mean they need letters of recommendations from academics. It is important that you not commit to writing a letter for someone is you do not have enough things to say to write a strong letter.

One of the most important things to remember about grad schools is that they are not just looking for students who will do well in the classroom. They are often looking for people who can work as teaching and research assistants and bring recognition to the school's program by their future achievements. They might also be looking for individuals who have new research ideas and show promise for being published. With that said, it is important to promote what the individual can offer the program and their fellow students as well as what they can do academically and professionally.

Example written by an Employer

I am writing to you on behalf of Debra Fletcher to recommend her for your MBA program. Debra has worked for me at ABC Consulting Comp. for five years. I hired her out of college as a Marketing Specialist and promoted her to Team Leader two years later.

Debra recently expressed her interest in pursuing an MBA so she can progress into roles of executive management. We have planned a schedule for her to pursue her MBA in your program while continuing in a consulting role with my company. I believe Debra is more than capable of excelling in both pursuits, but I am completely committed to adjusting her load as needed to facilitate her academics.

Over the last five years, I have found Debra to be innovative and highly-focused on customer needs. She demonstrates a keen ability to evaluate client requirements and transform them into effective marketing campaigns with high return-on-investment. She astutely manages resources and budgets without losing the creative aspects of marketing.

I believe Debra will prove to be a dedicated student who can offer her classmates insight on aspects related to marketing and customer relations. I highly encourage you to admit her to your MBA program, and if I can provide you any additional information, please let me know. You can reach me at 555-555-5555 or at jamesmichaelscott@ emailaddress.com.

Example written by a Teacher

It is my pleasure to write to you on behalf of Melody Burger, recommending her for your graduate program in Political Science. My first impression of Melody came as a stand-out student in a large lecture for American Federal Government. I had the opportunity to get to know her better in my Presidential Politics course her junior year.

Even though Melody was majoring in journalism, she excelled in her political analysis, research, and studies. She made thoughtful and insightful contributions to class discussion, indicating that she did more than just the required reading for the course. Additionally, I found her paper submissions to be comprehensive and high quality, particularly her submission on the relationships between the media and president's press secretaries.

Since Melody expressed an interest in political campaigning, I recommended her for an internship with a local candidate. His feedback on her work ethic and contributions was excellent, and he served as a source for her honor thesis on impartial media coverage of politicians and parties.

I highly endorse Melody for your graduate program and believe she will prove an asset to your university. If I can provide you with any additional information or be of any further assistance in your consideration of Melody's candidacy, please feel free to contact me at the phone or email listed above. Thank you for your time and consideration.

Scholarships/Fellowships

Scholarships and fellowships can require an application process and have set qualifications candidates need to meet. These can be academic in nature or speak to the character of the applicant. If you have been asked to write a letter of recommendation for this purpose, remember that funding can be essential to a person's academic pursuits. Also, the person is likely to be up against strong competition for this award, so take your time to highlight the candidate. Consider the following suggestions:

- The candidate's grades, sports achievements, and awards
- Leadership roles the candidate has held - sports captains, club presidents, other leadership roles
- The candidate's academic and professional goals
- Community service the candidate has completed
- Jobs the candidate has held and related achievements
- Achievements the candidate has contributed to in clubs or community organizations (fundraising results, special events, service projects)
- Financial needs
- Endorsement of how well the candidate will perform in school

Internships

While some might consider an internship an "entry-level" position, since some are tied to grades and not all of them are paid, I included it in the academic portion of this book. Letters of recommendation for internships can be completed by both professors and current or former part-time employers, but they need to speak to both academic and professional traits.

Internships are very important because they help new graduates present professional qualifications when they enter the job market at large. A letter of recommendation for an internship will help hiring managers choose from dozens or maybe hundreds of applicants. While you will want to talk about their academic success, I recommend you focus on other highlights to distinguish them from their competition. Consider:

- The candidate's future work goals
- The candidate's passion for the subject of the internship
- The candidate's achievements outside of academia such as work or community service
- The candidate's organizational skills, ability to deliver on a deadline, ability to perform under pressure
- The candidate's ability to do the internship -link what you know about the candidate to what you know the internship will require

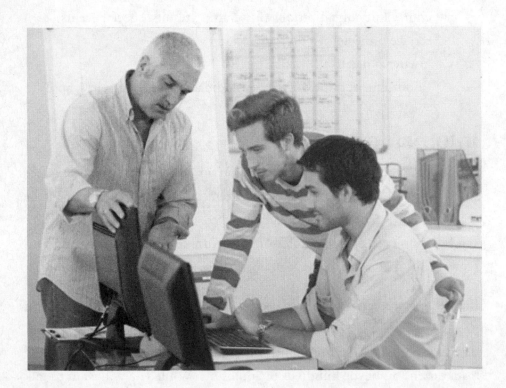

Chapter 9

Writing a Letter of Recommendation for a Friend

The personal letter of recommendation can be written for someone pursuing a professional or academic goal, but your relationship with him or her is a casual or friendly nature as opposed to the candidate being a professional associate or instructor. You might know a personal contact through a professional organization, a community service group, a church group, a parent/teacher association, a youth sports league, a Chamber of Commerce, and many other social settings.

For this reason, how you know or relate to the person might not reveal to you much of their professional life. You should ask them for a copy of their resume just to get to know them a bit on this front once you agree to write a letter of recommendation. You should also examine what transferable skills you have witnessed them use that you can speak about in your letter. The following is a brief list of things you can include in a professional letter of recommendation. Consider how many of them you can talk about even though you know the candidate in a personal way:

- Have they developed something new?
- Have they improved performance or a process?
- What do you remember most about this person?
- Are they always on time?
- Are they known as a person whom you can turn to when you need help?
- Do they have great interpersonal skills?
- Do they adapt to change easily?
- How does this person lead/manage?
- How does this person work with others or build collaboration?
- In what type of environment does this person perform best?
- What type of work ethic does this person have?
- How well does the candidate perform under pressure?

Just because your relationship with an individual is in a non-business setting does not mean you cannot write about skills the person has demonstrated which translate effectively to the job or school program they are pursuing. You need to spend time examining your interactions with the letter recipient and how you can translate your experience with that person to the skill sets the job or skill is looking to fill.

Fundraising activities can translate to proof of sales skills.

The fundraising event you saw the subject of your letter organize and manage demonstrates skills sets from event management to marketing and sales. Use specific examples from this type of work and make the connection for the reader to the type of work you think the recipient of the letter would do well in as a result.

Example:

> *Jane was a key part of our efforts to raise more than $2K for the local effort to provide Thanksgiving meals to needy families. She baked and sold hundreds of cookies for fundraising events held every other Saturday for three months prior to the meal drive. I believe this demonstrates a strong commitment to achieving organizational goals and stellar sales capabilities.*

Membership drives can demonstrate success in recruiting.

If the subject of your letter demonstrates an exceptional ability to bring in new members to your organization and build participation among your base, this can translate into a talent for recruiting and employee engagement.

Example:

> *During the time that John directed our membership drives, our organization grew by 20 percent and furthermore, more of our members participated in our social and community service events. Given John's interest in human resources, I believe this demonstrates an ability to effectively recruit, develop, and engage a large workforce.*

Working on building projects for a community service organization can showcase resource/project/budget management skills.

Whether the person organized an event for a group like Habitat for Humanity or just simply participated, he/she may have demonstrated skills that are transferable to his/her professional ambitions. If you are writing a letter of recommendation for a friend with whom you volunteered in this regards, you can use his/her management of resources or his/her ability to manage the budget while shopping for supplies as examples of transferable skills.

The bottom line is that you should include examples of achievements and interactions in your letter of recommendation that can speak specifically to what kind of professional or academic success the subject of your letter will achieve. You can use any number of subjects – organization of a church mission trip or policy development that was adopted by your local home owner's association – to communicate their skills and abilities. As long as you make the link, you will be fine.

Networking/
Introduction Letter

Much of this book has concentrated on letters of recommendation that will be printed and mailed or at least sent via attachment. This chapter, on the other hand, focuses on the electronic medium of professional networking and tools that sites like LinkedIn offer professionals to assist them in their networking and job search efforts. It also will provide recommendations for making networking connections if you are asked to do so by a friend or associate.

These networking or introduction letters are more casual than the letters of recommendation that I have covered so far, but they are still professional communications and can open doors for people's career pursuits. In short, they are important, but not as formal as the previous letters covered in this book.

Professional Networking Sites

Even with a free membership, LinkedIn offers the ability to view your connections' connections or perform searches for people working at certain companies so you can identify anyone in your circle who might work at a company you are targeting for employment.

As a result of these services, LinkedIn members can find themselves wanting to connect with someone they have never met before, but one of their connections knows. To do so, LinkedIn has established a "get connected" option where you request an introduction from your mutual associate.

While LinkedIn provides an option where you can use a default message, I strongly recommend personalizing the message a bit. Consider the examples below:

Dear John,

Hi there! I hope this note finds you doing well. In the process of examining opportunities for my next professional endeavor, I saw that you are connected to Mr./Ms. Smith from Company Name. I am highly interested in the work that Company Name is doing and would like to setup an information interview with someone in their organization.

For that purpose, would you be so kind as to arrange an introduction for me to Mr./Ms. Smith on LinkedIn? Of course, if you do not feel close enough to Mr./Ms. Smith to do so, I understand. I appreciate your time today and look forward to catching up with you soon.

Sincerely,

Your Name

Dear John,

Hi there! I hope this note finds you doing well. I am contacting you today because while evaluating my next professional opportunity, I noticed you are employed at one of my chief companies of interest. I am very interested in the work being done by Company Name (I would add an example here or personalize this more) and would like to meet with someone about opportunities there that might align well with my skill set.

If you would feel comfortable assisting me, could you recommend a good contact to meet with and/or arrange an introduction over Linked In? Of course, if you do not feel well enough connected with the right hiring authority, I understand. I appreciate your time today and look forward to catching up with you soon.

Sincerely,

Your Name

Once you receive this invitation like the ones listed above, if you decide you are willing to introduce your two connections on the website, you may select the appropriate response button and type a message to the recipient of the introduction. You should follow many of the same recommendations made throughout this book, but abbreviate the effort. Consider the following example:

Megan,

I am writing you to introduce you to my associate Bill Jones who worked with me on the construction project I told you about last year. He is interested in hearing about the work you are doing at Company Name and was hoping to meet with you briefly in those regards. I have arranged an introduction here on LinkedIn and leave it to you both to connect. If I can answer any questions for you regarding Bill, please just let me know.

Sincerely,

Your Name

Note to Applicants

While LinkedIn provides a template for you to fill out, it is a basic one at best. I recommend writing a longer note which includes an explanation to why you want the introduction and an expression of gratitude if they are able to help you in this regard. Of course, you should leave them an opportunity to decline.

Introductory Emails

If a friend of yours is interested in working for your company, but you do not know enough about his or her professional work to provide them a letter of recommendation, you can still serve as a networking contact. In an instance like this, you might be asked to pass along their resume and ask the hiring manager to consider the applicant for an interview.

Another example where you might need to put together an introductory email is when a recent graduate you know demonstrates an interest in your industry or specific company. In this case, you might be asked to refer the candidate to the appropriate hiring manager for an "informational" interview. This is an interview where the person sits down to learn about the job/company/industry that they are interested in pursuing without specifically applying for a job opening.

In either of these cases, if you are asked to refer the candidate, you will need to write a quick email explaining how you know the candidate, what you can recommend about the candidate, the candidate's contact information, and an offer to answer any questions the person might have before they respond to the candidate. Consider the following examples:

John,

Hi there! My friend Paul Williams has just moved here from Wyoming and wants to get a beat on the area job market in technology sales. I know he has been a top performer at his former company and while he is new to the area, I know he has a lot to offer his next employer. If you can meet with him next week and provide him any solid job leads, I would really appreciate it. I have attached his resume to this email for you to review. If I can answer any additional questions, please just let me know.

Sincerely,

Your Name

Kendra,

I am dropping you a quick note regarding my niece who recently graduated with her Bachelor's in Marketing from State University. She is very interested in working in-house for a cosmetic company like ours and would like to meet with you to learn about our marketing operation. Janice is a creative mind and won a few school awards for impactful use of social media. I would appreciate any help or references you can give her for her job search.

I have attached her resume to this email and you can reach her at 555-555-5555. If you have any questions for me, please feel free to email or call me at the number listed below.

Sincerely,

Your Name

Chapter 11

Performance Evaluations

performance evaluation can act as a sort of internal letter of recommendation with the exception that the recipient does not get to choose who writes it and you cannot politely decline. However, much of what is in this book including recommendations on protecting yourself from negative backlash can still apply.

In *199 Pre-Written Employee Performance Appraisals: The Complete Guide to Successful Employee Evaluations & Documentation* authors Stephanie Lyster and Anne Arthur detail excellent procedures for the entire employee evaluation process.

In this book, they describe several rating systems which should prove helpful not only in performance evaluations but in brainstorming the basis of all letters of recommendation. If your company does not have a pre-set method for employee evaluations, the overview to using one of two common rating systems that follows provides beneficial information.

Three-Level Systems

A three-level rating system is simple and easy to use. It places employees in one of the following categories:

1. Exceeds Expectations
2. Meets Expectations
3. Needs Improvement

From school teachers to employers, many people find this system to be an easy way to evaluate a person's performance. However, it might allow too many people to fall into one category and therefore not create enough distinction between team members.

Five-Level Systems

The five-level rating system provides employees the greatest feedback on their performance. It also enables managers to distinguish between exceptional performance, good performance, and average performance:

1. Exceeds Expectations
2. Above Average
3. Average
4. Below Average
5. Needs Improvement

Each of these can be flushed out to provide the employee with greater detail about his/her performance.

If you need to create a formal appraisal form for your direct reports, be sure to include the following information.

- Employee Name
- Title
- Review Date
- Supervisor Name
- Rating System Description
- List of Skills and Responsibilities – Rating and Comments
- Major Accomplishments
- Areas for Improvement
- Training and Development Plan
- Employee Comments
- Signatures: Employee and Rater

NOTE

If you have been asked to and agreed to write a professional letter of recommendation, performance evaluations could be a good source of information to re-familiarize yourself with things you have noted about the employee in the past and their major accomplishments. You can also make note if they have improved upon their performance over the years and if training and development plans have been effective. All of this information could prove valuable for your letter writing efforts.

Chapter 12

What to Leave Out of a Letter of Recommendation

*A*s mentioned previously throughout this book, there are specific topics and certain ideas you should avoid in letters of recommendation. To ensure this topic is given enough consideration, a quick reference guide that you can switch to when writing the letter itself is included. Remember, the following are items that if mentioned, could hamper or eliminate a candidate from consideration. Tread lightly with each of the following subject areas:

Do not mention negatives.

First, though I have seen it mentioned in other letter of recommendation guides, I do not advocate including negatives. Executive Career Coach Valerie El-Jamil agrees: "If you have a negative that someone wants to address, you will want them to talk about how you overcame it. It is nice to show that you have the ability to grow. I always tell my clients to not let a negative hang over their head, but to show that it has been corrected.

I once had a client with a personal bankruptcy who was working in the financial industry. He had received two or three job offers and he did not mention it to any of them until it came out late in the job search process. The offers were all withdrawn. This is just one example of how it can be bad not to address a negative during the interview process.

However, it can be problematic for you to address these things for a person. What is better is if you can talk about a negative in terms of your relationship with the person while describing how the relationship changed and a negative was turned into a positive."

The bottom line of talking about negatives is that you do not want to mention anything in the letter of recommendation that will hurt the person's candidacy. If you bring up a negative, but do not address it well enough, you could distract from the positives you are going over in the letter. The hiring manager will expect a very strong letter and frequent mention of negatives will not serve to achieve that.

Do not make references to things the hiring manager is not allowed to ask.

While you will naturally refer to the candidate as male or female by using the appropriate pronouns, you should avoid specific references to things a hiring manager is not allowed to ask about the candidate. These include references to the candidate's age, race, religion, or sexual orientation.

Depending on how well you know the candidate, it might come naturally to discuss the time you spend together at some church organization or another club with strong implications regarding one of these subject areas. But these are things a hiring manager is specifically not allowed to ask about and if the candidate does not want them revealed, you should probably not mention them in your letter.

If you want to address a disability of the candidate's, like impaired hearing or vision, and how the candidate overcomes that perceived negative to perform with excellence would be acceptable for a letter of recommendation. However, I would still advise that you review that with the person you are writing the letter for first.

Do not reveal information about the candidate's current salary or salary needs.

If you are the candidate's manager or former manager, you might know things about his/her salary or salary requirements others would not know. Be sure not to make reference to such details in your letter of recommendation.

Career coaches advise their clients not to discuss salary until the interview process, and whenever possible to let the hiring manager make the first offer. While the candidate must know their salary needs, they will want to keep that information to themselves until they can get an idea of what the hiring manager can offer.

Salary negotiations should be delayed until the candidate is able to make a positive impression on the hiring manager and secure his/her place in the consideration process. Your letter should not divulge or hint at information that might put the candidate at a disadvantage when negotiating his/her pay.

> Salary negotiations should be delayed until the candidate is able to make a positive impression on the hiring manager and secure his/her place in the consideration process.

Negative implications can range from talking about how the candidate always won bonuses -they might offer a lower base salary if they think the individual can increase their pay through bonuses - to indicating that the person's spouse just landed a high paying job that moved them across country away from your business. It is good to state that they are leaving for positive reasons and you would keep them if you could; you should not make it seem like they do not need to make as much because their spouse has a high salary.

While there are positives associated with saying the candidate was a top-rated, award-winning performer or that the only reason the candidate is leaving you is because their partner was transferred to another state, it is important to phrase these facts carefully so there is no negative impact on potential pay.

Avoid references to politically "hot" topics.

Certain clubs and activities carry specific intonations and whether these implications are positive or negative can vary depending on what part of the US in which you live or work. Additionally, political affiliations, like political parties and interest groups, can bring with them a heap of preconceived ideas and assumptions. You should consider where the person is applying for work and how the group or activity might be seen in that part of the country. Consider the following examples:

- It might be ok to talk about being a member of the National Rifle Association (NRA) in certain states, but that affiliation would raise red flags to hiring managers in other locations.

- You should remove references to political parties and candidate support in areas that are largely dominated by members of the opposite party. It might even be a bad idea to keep it on in areas dominated strongly by member of your own party; politics is just never a good topic for an interview.

- It is advisable to remove references to organizations that support certain emotionally-charged policy topics such as Planned Parenthood or pro-life groups because you never know when such an affiliation could cause a reader to unconscientiously overlook a candidate.

If part of the reason you know a candidate is work you did together on a political campaign or through an organization that might have some political charge to it, be sure to focus on the achievements or work you completed together as opposed to the group you belonged.

Minimize references to things that would distract from the person's work.

Even if you know the candidate is moving to care for ailing parents, it might not be a good idea to be extremely detailed in explaining what is taking the person away from your employment. It is important that a hiring manager feel like the candidate will give their job 100 percent of their time and effort. If you spend a great deal of time emphasizing the importance of family and children and how this takes up in the candidate's life, you might get him/her overlooked for a hire.

You can reference a candidate moving for family reasons or being a dedicated parent, but always emphasize how they excel in their work as they balance it with the personal life. Make sure that you are clear how professional the candidate is and how he/she produce solid results. While people always talk about wanting well-rounded employees, they still do not want to feel like anything might take away from the candidate giving work their full effort.

PART THREE

*T*he third section of the book provides a large overview of sample letters of recommendations, including several different professions, academic pursuits, and networking situations.

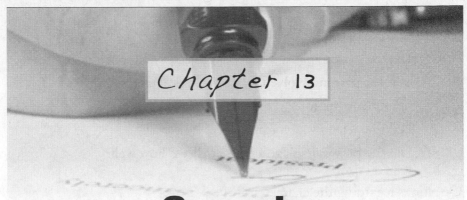

Chapter 13

Sample Professional Letters of Recommendation

Chapters 6 and 7 explained the strategies and content you should consider when writing a professional letter of recommendation, including the relationship you hold with the subject of the letter, that person's level of experience, and whether the position is for another company or for an internal opening. This chapter contains several sample letters that work to answer some combination of the following:

Questions regarding how the person performed their job:

- Did the person save the company money?
- Did the person make the company money?
- Did the person help develop new products for the company?

- Did the person improve company processes?
- Did the person manage a special project, event, opening, or closing?
- Was the person involved in technological upgrades or implementations?
- Did the person lead a team? If yes how well?
- Did the person manage a budget? If yes how well?

Questions regarding the character of the person:

- Is this person consistently on time?
- Does this person take on extra work or put in more effect to ensure the job is done well?
- Does this person support or help their coworkers?
- Does the person relate well with coworkers, clients, and managers?
- What characteristics would you say describe the person?
- How does this person distinguish themselves as an employee?
- Does this person deal well with change?
- What type of corporate culture does this person work best in?

Questions relating to your relationship with the subject of the letter:

- What impresses you most about the candidate?
- How have you seen the person grow or change as an employee?
- Would you hire/rehire the individual? Or would you work for the individual again?

You do not need to answer all of these questions in one single letter of recommendation, but you should try to answer several together as you talk about the candidate. But please note, of all the questions you can try to answer in your letter, be sure to express that you would hire or retain or work with the candidate again if you had the option. This will resonant with the reader.

Professional Letter of Recommendation
Written by Current or Former Employer (Management)

MICHAEL COLLINS

555-555-5555 | Street Address, City, State, Zip | michaelcollins@emailaddress.com

(Date)

Mr. (Ms.) _____
(Company)

(Address 1)
(Address 2)

Dear Mr. (Ms.) _____:

I am writing you on behalf of Jason Smith, who has asked me to serve as a reference for him. Mr. Smith works for me at the XYZ Public Charter School of Washington in Washington, DC, and I have had the opportunity to partner with him on many assignments.

Mr. Smith has an excellent work ethic and response time, regularly going above and beyond the duties of his position. It is not uncommon for me to see him on my campus at night or on weekends, resolving some technical issue that others might have put off. He also provided me valuable collaboration of the school's IT budget, helping devise a way to meet the school's immediate technology needs as well as developing a strategic plan for an enterprise IT refresh and augmentation.

Mr. Smith maintains operating and capital IT budgets for the schools, provides system administration, and delivers tier III support when needed. He also provided a valuable contribution when he installed and configured web-filters that insured compliance with federal regulations.

Having demonstrated commitment and passion for his work and solid leadership abilities, I believe Mr. Smith is a natural choice for a senior management position and I support his efforts for career advancement. I am confident he would be as much of an asset to your organization as he has been to XYZ and I strongly recommend him to you.

I will gladly answer any additional questions you might have and you can reach me at 555-555-5555 for a personal interview if needed.

Sincerely,

Michael Collins
Head of School XYZ

Professional Letter of Recommendation
Written by Current or Former Employer (Project Manager)

JENNIFER L. JONES

555-555-5555 | Street Address, City, State, Zip | jenniferljones@emailaddress.com

(Date)

Mr. (Ms.) _____
Title
(Company)
(Address 1)
(Address 2)

Dear Mr. (Ms.) _____:

Letter of Reference for Jacob Smith

Jacob Smith has asked me to write to you recommending his work as a project manager for my company, Construction Services, Inc. It is my pleasure to give him the highest recommendation for his project management, client relations, and budgetary skills.

Jacob has been an asset in planning and executing high value government and commercial contracts. His experience in the US Army's Core of Engineers gives him an edge in working with military personnel and he quickly became my go-to-guy for defense contracts in the southeastern United States.

One of Jacob's greatest strengths is his ability to bring contractors, subcontractors, city/state agency representatives, and other stakeholders together in an efficient effort to carry out a client's needs. He always delivered his projects on-time and typically under budget, but I have to say the skill that impressed me the most was his ability to deal with client's who micromanaged or frequently requested changes in the construction plan. He was always able to deliver high levels of service, no matter how extreme the client pressure got.

Over the last seven years, Jacob has enjoyed traveling for work and was one of the best on-site managers I could have asked for. Now that he and his wife are expecting their second child and they want to live closer to her ailing parents, Jacob has decided to look outside my organization for work so that he can settle in Dallas and focus his time in the Dallas/Fort Worth area.

While my team will miss Jacob, I can assure you that my loss would be your gain, and he will quickly prove to be a valuable member of your team. If I can be of any additional assistance as you consider Jacob's candidacy, please feel free to contact me at the phone or email address listed above.

Sincerely,

Jennifer L. Jones
President, Construction Services, Inc.

Professional Letter of Recommendation
Written by Current or Former Employer (Project Manager)

CASEY ANDERSON

555-555-5555 | Street Address, City, State, Zip | caseyanderson@emailaddress.com

(Date)

Mr. (Ms.) _____

Title

(Company)

(Address 1)

(Address 2)

Dear Mr. (Ms.) _____:

I am writing you on behalf of Michelle Ryan who has asked me to serve as a reference for her for your open position of project manager. Ms. Ryan has managed construction projects for me for several years, with assignments ranging from single family homes to multiuse ten-story buildings with multimillion dollar budgets and dozens of subcontractors.

It is with deep regret that I learned Ms. Ryan and her husband will be relocating and we will be sorry to lose her at Construction Services, Inc. Please allow me to provide you with a brief glimpse of her work and character:

- Managed 25 multimillion-dollar construction projects over a seven year period, directing several subcontractor relationships simultaneously.

- Works effectively with clients, from individual families to corporate CEOs/Boards; communicates with tenants to customize buildings/offices to ensure all technical and physical needs were met.

- Serves as go-to person to turn around delayed or troubled projects, adjusting for obstacles and weather issues to ensure on-time project delivery and full customer satisfaction.

While my team will miss Michelle, I can assure you that my loss would be your gain, and she will quickly prove to be a valuable member of your team. If I can be of any additional assistance as you consider Michelle's candidacy, please feel free to contact me at the phone or email address listed above.

Sincerely,

Casey Anderson
President, Construction Services, Inc.

Professional Letter of Recommendation
Written by Current or Former Employer (Marketing Executive)

ALAN SMITH, CEO, IT PRODUCTS, INC.

555-555-5555 ext. 555 | Company Name, Location |alansmith@ITproducts.com

(Date)

Mr. (Ms.) _____
Title
(Company)
(Address 1)
(Address 2)

Dear Mr. (Ms.) _____:

I am writing you today regarding Janice Jones's candidacy for marketing executive. Janice worked for me in my previous role at as vice president of sales & marketing for IT-R-Us, and I am pleased to recommend her for your company now.

During the time I worked with Janice, IT-R-Us realized some of their largest revenue gains in the telecom and business applications segments. Her creativity and understanding of customer perception allowed us to shape sales and marketing campaigns that garnered a great deal of consumer interests along these lines. We even received national news coverage in papers and industry magazines. Janice really went out of her way to work with the product development team to make sure our marketing message had substance – not just flash.

Janice is not just a creative force in the marketing department; she also has a keen understanding of business goals and bottom-lines. In five years, she delivered the highest ROI marketing work the company had seen. Janice accomplished this through a blend of traditional marketing strategies and social media/web-marketing that led record-numbers of web traffic to the corporate website. But she did not stop at getting people to the website. She also worked with IT to make sure the website was visually appealing, user friendly, and was optimized for e-commerce.

When I left IT-R-Us to found my current company with a long-time friend, I tried to persuade Janice to coming with me. Unfortunately for me, Janice feels more at home in a larger corporation. I believe her career aspirations align very well with your organization's needs. Since she is fluent in Spanish and French, I know she is particularly interested in leveraging her foreign language skills in your overseas operations.

I strongly endorse Janice's application for your company and I believe you will quickly consider her as valuable an asset as I did. If I can answer any additional questions, please contact me at the number or email address listed above. Thank you for your time and consideration.

Sincerely,

Alan Smith

Professional Letter of Recommendation
Written by Current or Former Employer (Management)

PATRICIA ROBINSON

Phone | Street Address, City, State, Zip | email address

(Date)

Mr. (Ms.) _____
(Company)
(Address 1)
(Address 2)

Dear Mr. (Ms.) _____:

Mr. Gary Smith has asked me to write you and serve as a reference for his application. I am more than happy to do so and can strongly recommend him for the work he does for me at ABC School of Georgia. I can personally attest to his work ethic, innovation, team leadership and project management skills.

As our Systems and IT Director, Mr. Smith worked with me on the technical aspects of large-scale constructions projects at the school that included a four-story dorm build, academic building remodel, and preparation of portable temporary classrooms.

While he was managing staff members and IT aspects of these projects, Mr. Smith accounted for ROI and scalability in the decision marketing process. The end result was an affordable IT upgrade for the campus that aligned with larger technology plans for the school.

Mr. Smith maintains operating and capital IT budgets for the schools, provides system administration, and delivers tier III support when needed. He excels in cross-functional collaboration, handling multiple assignments simultaneously, and delivering calm management under time and budget constraints.

I am confident he will prove to be a beneficial member of your organization as he has been for ours. I support his efforts for career advancements and encourage you to examine his application with interest. If you need to reach me for any additional questions, please feel free to call or email me at the contact information above.

Sincerely,

Patricia Robinson
COO ABC School of Georgia

Professional Letter of Recommendation
Written by Current or Former Employer (Accounting Director)

JOHN SMITH

Phone | Street Address, City, State, Zip | email address

(Date)

Mr. (Ms.) _____
Title
(Company)
(Address 1)
(Address 2)

Dear Mr. (Ms.) _____:

I am pleased to write this letter on behalf of William Jones, who worked with me in the financial department of Widgets Direct. As the CFO of an early stage company, I relied on my accounting director, William, immensely to ensure our domestic and international sales growth was fully compliant with all applicable regulations and tax codes.

I recruited William from a Big 4 Accounting agency and was very pleased with his contributions. His consultancy work parleyed into expert advice for us that helped us establish a business presence in 12 countries across Europe and Asia while doubling our revenue performance in the US.

When William told me he needed to move back to the East Coast for family reasons, I was disappointed to lose him. We are still realizing the benefit of his efforts as his protégé is continuing to meet our accounting needs. William's work ethic is top notch, and he continuously goes that extra mile to ensure that all accounting work is done completely and accurately.

As a manager, William recruited a solid team and took an interest in their professional development. Two of his staff earned their CPA licenses under his mentorship. William regularly led training sessions on financial management, tax code, and proper software utilization. The staff he recruited, developed, and mentored is still in tack and performing very well.

I highly recommend William for your open position and encourage you to consider him a valuable business partner. I can assure you that he will help you realize whatever growth objectives you have for your company while infusing your accounting/finance department with the highest levels of professional standards.

If I can provide any additional information for your consideration of William's candidacy, please let me know. I can be reached by phone at 555-555-5555 or email at jsmith@widgetsdirect.com.

Sincerely,

John Smith
Chief Financial Officer

Professional Letter of Recommendation
Written by Current or Former Employer (Finance Director)

LISA JONES

Phone | Street Address, City, State, Zip | email address

(Date)

Mr. (Ms.) _____

Title

(Company)

(Address 1)

(Address 2)

Dear Mr. (Ms.) _____:

I am pleased to write this letter on behalf of Bethany Smith who has been a vital member of my financial team at Acme XYZ for seven years. During this time, I have relied on her to ensure our US and international sales growth was achieved in full compliance with all applicable regulations and that our accounting functions were completed accurately and completely each year.

Highlights of her work include the following:

- Developed strategies for successful market penetration in South America and Eastern Europe.
- Hired and mentored financial and accounting managers to facilitate international growth.
- Enhanced profit margins 10 percent as the company increased revenue 25 percent.
- Fostered a collaborative work environment and highly engaged workforce.

When Bethany told me that her husband had been promoted and transferred out west, I knew I was losing a team member that would be incredibly hard to replace. I highly recommend Bethany for your open position of Finance Director and can assure you that she will help you realize whatever growth objectives you have for your company.

If I can provide any additional information for your consideration of Bethany's candidacy, please let me know. I can be reached by phone at 555-555-5555 or email at lisajones@acmexyz.com

Sincerely,

Lisa Jones
Chief Executive Officer

Professional Letter of Recommendation
Written by Current or Former Employer (Software Engineer)

JACK B. GOOD

Phone | Street Address, City, State, Zip | email address

(Date)

Mr. (Ms.) _____
Title
(Company)
(Address 1)
(Address 2)

Dear Mr. (Ms.) _____:

Letter of Reference for Michael Williams

I am writing you to recommend Michael Williams for the position of software development engineer. I managed Michael in my former role as vice president of product development for Major IT Company, Inc. During out time working together, Michael worked on developing five major releases and dozens of software updates.

Michael expertly managed the software development life cycle for his assigned products which, upon release, realized millions of dollars in revenue for our company. The product areas he worked on included financial management, banking, scheduling/calendar organization, and graphic design.

When I hired Michael, he was already well experienced in writing code, testing and debugging products, and user acceptance testing. He also proved himself a quick learner and easily adapted when our company transitioned to Agile methodologies. Always eager to expand his expertise and credentials, Michael studied for and gained his certification through IEEE under my management.

I found Michael to be a consummate professional, delivering assignments on-time and in complete adherence to pre-set requirements. He also worked well with client and sales representatives to create product updates that responded to demands of our customers.

I believe Major IT Company benefited from Michael's employment and you will as well. If I can answer any additional questions about his qualifications, expertise, or achievements, I will be happy to do so. Please just contact me at 555-555-5555 or jackbgood@emailaddress.com.

Sincerely,

Jack B. Good

Professional Letter of Recommendation
Written by Current or Former Employer (Sales Manager)

JESSICA ANNE SMITH

555-555-5555 | Street Address, City, State, Zip | jessicaannesmith@emailaddress.com

(Date)

Mr. (Ms.) _____
Title
(Company)
(Address 1)
(Address 2)

Dear Mr. (Ms.) _____:

Ms. Ayla Jones has asked me to serve as a reference on her behalf, and I am writing to you to strongly recommend her to lead your sales organization in Florida. She is an energetic sales professional who has expressed a strong interest in representing your company. I believe she will bring a passion for promoting your product that extends beyond a desire to make quota or commission.

When I worked with Ayla at Major Retail Company, Inc., she loved our products and was better than any sales commercial when it came to getting customers excited our their purchases. She exceeded her sales targets most quarters and was a pivotal part of making sure my store was rated highest in the nation for revenue dollars, customer service, and client retention.

At Major Retail Company, Inc., Ayla headed my line of jewelry products. She had a unique way of pairing products to customer wants and budgets. On one occasion, I received a glowing letter of commendation for her from a bride who she helped pick out her bridesmaid's gifts and accessories. We did not have anything in the store the bride really wanted, but rather than lose the sale to another store, Ayla poured through some catalogs to find the perfect products. That client spent thousands of dollars with us and completed a bridal registry with us when she did not originally plan to do so. It is that ability to change a one-time sale into a long-term client that makes Ayla truly special.

Since our time working together, Ayla earned an MBA and held two management positions. Even when she was working for me, I could see she had a talent for managing and training staff. I believe the combination of her sales and leadership talent will make her a fine additional to your sales organization. Additionally, she has a rich network in the state of Florida having spent her childhood there and attended the University of Florida for her MBA.

I highly recommend Ayla for your Sales Director position in Florida. I believe she will make an immediate impact on your top lines and infuse a positive energy into your sales team. If I can be of any additional assistance as you evaluate her candidacy, please let me know. Thank you for your time.

Best Regards,

Jessica Anne Smith

Professional Letter of Recommendation
Written by Current or Former Employer (Logistics Supervisor)

JONATHAN A. WEBB

555-555-5555 | Street Address, City, State, Zip | jonathanawebb@emailaddress.com

(Date)

Mr. (Ms.) _____
Title
(Company)
(Address 1)
(Address 2)

Dear Mr. (Ms.) _____:

Letter of Reference for Timothy Jones

I am writing to you to recommend Timothy Jones for your logistics supervisor opening. Timothy gained experience in warehouse management and supply chain planning while working for me at ACME, Inc. He proved himself to be an excellent planner and detailed organizer for inventory, shipping and receiving, and warehousing of a wide-range of products, including ones needing special environmental storage.

Timothy was hired as a supply chain specialist to plan delivery routes for chemical products via land, air, and sea. He did an excellent job of ensuring his routes were executed well and delivered on-time while adhering to budget constraints. He is also trained on OSHA requirements and ensured full regulatory compliance for all delivery efforts.

I promoted Timothy to warehouse supervisor and most recently to warehouse manager and could not be more proud of the work he has performed. He manages the processing and storage of tens of thousands of products daily with collective value in the seven-figure range. He has also proven himself to be a solid recruiter, trainer, and union liaison. We employ union and non-union employees, salaried, full-time, and part-time workers as well as contract drivers. Timothy manages their performance effectively while handling any disciplinary problems with complete professionalism. He is highly rated by his peers and direct reports.

While I would love to keep Timothy in-house, he has expressed a strong interest in moving closer to his parents. Your logistics office in Georgia would be an ideal fit for him, and I believe he will prove a strong asset for your company. I appreciate the time you have spent reading this letter. If I can provide any additional information while you consider Timothy's application, please contact me at the contact information listed above.

Sincerely,

Jonathan A. Webb

Professional Letter of Recommendation
Written by Current or Former Employer (HR Generalist)

ROBERT WILLIAMS

555-555-5555 | emailaddress.com

(Date)

Mr. (Ms.) _____
Title
(Company)
(Address 1)
(Address 2)

Dear Mr. (Ms.) _____:

Janice Langston has asked me to recommend her for your open position of human resources generalist, and it my pleasure to do so. Janice has been working for my company for ten years, covering the dual role of HR Manager and Office Administrator. I am now looking at retiring and even though my son is taking over the business, Janice wants to work for a larger company.

I hired Janice after she completed her bachelor's degree in human resources management with the University of Tennessee. She worked with me while my company acquired a competitor and experienced 150 percent growth. Her knowledge of employment laws, workers' compensation, and other relevant regulations has proven invaluable during these periods of change.

Janice has proven invaluable in analyzing and selecting benefits plans for our employees and communicating the details of those plans and any relevant changes to our staff. She has also recommended and implemented two upgrades to our personnel and payroll management systems. As a result, she is highly qualified in applications such as QuickBooks and PeopleSoft.

To ensure we had highly qualified and credentialed staff, Janice focused on organizing training events and facilitating professional development for our employees. As a result, she has empowered three employees to complete Six Sigma Green Belt certifications, helped our project management personnel complete PMP certifications, and arranged for one of my managers to complete his MBA.

As the office administrator, Janice professionally handled employee, client, and vendor communications and managed office staff personnel. I highly recommend her for your human resources generalist role and will happily provide any additional information if you need it. Thank you for your time and consideration.

Sincerely,

Robert Williams

Professional Letter of Recommendation
Written by Current or Former Employer (Graphic Designer)

ANDREW R. JOHNSON

555-555-5555 | Street Address, City, State, Zip | andrewrjohnson@emailaddress.com

(Date)

Mr. (Ms.) _____
Title
(Company)
(Address 1)
(Address 2)

Dear Mr. (Ms.) _____:

Letter of Recommendation for Mary Smith

I am writing you to recommend Mary Smith for your open role of Graphics Designer. You will find her a highly creative professional who completes her assignments in full compliance with client requirements and budget/timeline constraints. Mary excels in translating project and client needs into visually compelling pieces of graphic design.

As a Marketing Manager with XYZ Corporation, I found Mary's assistance in creating print collateral and pieces for customer communications invaluable. After working with Mary for a year, I gave her control of a $50K budget for software, technology, and training and development. She managed it effectively while improving the quality of her four-member team tenfold.

Mary oversaw the addition of MAC computers, Adobe Creative Suites, and an internship program with a nearby university and community college. For the internship program, Mary selected one paid intern in the fall and spring to work on our team and two to three unpaid interns to work on short-term client projects in the summer. The students gained valuable insight, and we benefited from the creativity and innovation of youthful minds.

In addition to her print work, Mary made several contributions to our web page and social media pages. In one instance, she designed a Facebook ad that garnered tens of thousands of hits and increased our website orders 10 percent.

I left XYZ Corporation in 2010 to take a higher executive role with a larger company. From what the CEO tells me, Mary continued to make excellent contributions after I left. Now she tells me she wants to work in a different industry and concentrate on digital/web design. I believe she will be a strong asset to you in this arena and I fully endorse her application. If I can be of any additional assistance, please contact me at 555-555-5555 or andrewrjohnson@emailaddress.com.

Sincerely,

Andrew R. Johnson

Professional Letter of Recommendation
Written by Current or Former Employer (Restaurant Manager)

MICHELLE LEE SMITH

555-555-5555 | Street Address, City, State, Zip | mlsmith@emailaddress.com

(Date)

Mr. (Ms.) _____
Title
(Company)
(Address 1)
(Address 2)

Dear Mr. (Ms.) _____:

Alex Hernandez has asked me to write to you on his behalf, recommending him for the role of Restaurant Manager for your new location in Miami, Florida. I have had the privilege of working with Alex in two locations, once when he was a chef and again when he was the Catering Coordinator at my current restaurant. I find him to be an excellent judge of menu selection and pricing as well as a rock solid kitchen/event manager.

Alex left my current restaurant team last year when he needed to commit to school full-time to complete his Bachelor's, and while I would love to have him back, he tells me he is committed to living in Miami with his fiancé. As a result, I believe my loss is your gain! Alex will not just run your restaurant well; he delights your clientele and builds a strong base of regulars in no time. His customer service is top-notch, and I frequently received compliments on his work from our patrons.

In addition to these skills, Alex also excels in running budgets and teams. He ensures his staff members are all certified in food safety and trained on the most recent laws and regulations. He also keeps them – bartenders in particular – knowledgeable of drink and dietary trends so they can answer customer questions with confidence and expertise.

I fully endorse Alex's application for your Restaurant Manager and will be happy to answer any additional questions you might have of me. I appreciate the time you have taken to read this letter. If needed, please contact me at the phone number or email listed above.

Best Regards,

Michelle Lee Smith

Professional Letter of Recommendation
Written by Current or Former Employer (Benefits Coordinator)

DAVID L. SMITH

555-555-5555 | emailaddress.com

(Date)

Mr. (Ms.) _____
Title
(Company)
(Address 1)
(Address 2)

Dear Mr. (Ms.) _____:

Letter of Recommendation for Wendy Wu

I am writing you on behalf of Wendy Wu to endorse her application for your open role of Benefits Coordinator. Wendy is a highly skilled human resources professional with comprehensive experience in payroll management, vendor relations, and benefits selection/administration. She has worked for me for five years, running our sales commission program and 401 (k) Plan.

Wendy accurately tracks sales performance for 150 sales representatives across the US, monitoring them against their budgeted plan to identify who has made their sales quotas, earned commissions, and will receive designation in the President's Club each year. This involves tracking millions of dollars in sales revenue and awarding tens of thousands of dollars in bonuses, and Wendy performs this task without error.

When it comes to managing our 401 (k) Plan, Wendy selected the financial provider that we use and ensures accurate administration for 300+ company employees. In the past, Wendy has handled our payroll function and health insurance benefits. Two years ago, when we merged with a competitor, we slightly expanded our HR team and made Wendy's role more specialized.

Though your organization is larger, I believe Wendy will prove highly capable of directing your benefits plan. She has a strong desire to work for a *Fortune* 500 company and thinks very highly of your products and services. I recommend you consider her further for this role and would be happy to answer any additional questions you might have. Please feel free to contact me at 555-555-5555 or email me at davidlsmith@email.com.

Sincerely,

David L. Smith

Professional Letter of Recommendation
Written by Current or Former Coworker (Sales & Marketing Exe)

DIANE LINDA SMITH

555-555-5555 | emailaddress.com

(Date)

Mr. (Ms.) _____

Title

(Company)

(Address 1)

(Address 2)

Dear Mr. (Ms.) _____:

Letter of Reference for George Smith

I am pleased to write to you on behalf of George Smith, recommending him for your position of Sales and Marketing Executive. Prior to my promotion to Client Relations Manager, I worked for George for four years and found him to be an excellent manager and mentor.

While I was working for George, our department grew company revenue 30 percent year-after-year, and a large part of our success was his commitment to identifying sales strategies that generated the best results and communicating them to our entire team. At times, we had to change the way we approached our clients or presented our products, but each change improved our sales numbers.

George set the highest standards for himself and routinely worked with us one-on-one to help us achieve our sales quotas. As a team, we ranked highest in the company for sales and customer service, and George was always the top-rated manager in the country. When he was promoted to Sales and

Marketing Vice President, he coached me to assume my new role in client relations. Though I was no longer his direct report, I still found him to be a strong leader and mentor.

Outside of our sales work, George placed a strong emphasis on community service and regularly organized employee participation in charity events. He excelled in creating strong corporate ties to the community and positive public perception. I highly recommend him for your company and believe he will be a strong asset to your leadership team. Thank you for your time and consideration.

Sincerely,

Diane Linda Smith

Professional Letter of Recommendation
Written by Current or Former Coworker (Operations Manager)

REBECCA L. ROBINSON

555-555-5555 | Street Address, City, State, Zip | lrobinson@emailaddress.com

(Date)

Mr. (Ms.) _____
Title
(Company)
(Address 1)
(Address 2)

Dear Mr. (Ms.) _____:

I am pleased to write to you on behalf of Shane Taylor, recommending him for your open position of Operations Manager. I have worked with Shane at Widgets-R-Us for five years and can attest to his ability to effectively run a production floor in a manufacturing environment. My job has been to oversee the safety and environmental compliance functions of our operation, and Shane always supported my efforts.

While I worked to achieve and maintain ISO certifications, Shane organized training sessions to ensure our new policies and procedures were understood and adhered to by more than 100 production floor workers over three shifts. Despite stricter regulations, Shane was able to increase his production numbers and quality ratings during the same period.

As a manager, Shane is a well-respected, hands-on leader who arrives early and leaves late. He shows his employees that he gives as much as he demands and takes an active role in mentoring his assistant managers. He also believes in making sure production equipment is well maintained, and I often worked with him to decide when machines and tools needed to refurbished or replaced.

I believe Shane will make an immediate, positive difference in your organization, and I highly endorse his application. If I can answer any additional questions about Shane's work, please feel free to call me on my cell at 555-555-5555 or email me on my personal account at beckyr@email.com. Thank you for your time.

Best Regards,

Rebecca L. Robinson

Professional Letter of Recommendation
Written by Current or Former Coworker (IT Team Leader)

Christopher M. Williams

555-555-5555 | Street Address, City, State, Zip | cmwilliam@emailaddress.com

(Date)

Mr. (Ms.) _____
Title
(Company)
(Address 1)
(Address 2)

Dear Mr. (Ms.) _____:

Letter of Recommendation for Sidney Jones

Sidney Jones requested that I write to you on his behalf, recommending him for your open position of IT Team Leader. I have been working with Sidney for the past year on a software development project for Major Financial Client. When Sidney joined the team, he was not the official leader, but he did take the lead in turning around our lagging, over budget project.

Our assignment has changed project managers three times since its inception and this created a sense of discontinuity and a software program that was not meeting the needs of our client's end-users. Sidney came on the project and brought us together to identify where were we missing the user requirements and formulate a plan to correct the issues. Without any special pay or recognition, Sidney got us back on track, and we delivered the program this month to a very pleased client.

I would describe Sidney as a hard-working, innovative, cost-conscious problem solver. Aside from working on our project, Sidney helped identify areas where our team and other department personnel could benefit from additional training. He successfully organized training sessions for employees to complete certifications, including instruction on Agile development methods.

I believe you would benefit from Sidney's technical and leadership expertise and highly recommend him for your company. I appreciate the time you have spent reading this letter. If you need any additional information regarding Sidney, please feel free to contact me at the phone or email listed above.

Sincerely,

Christopher M. Williams

Professional Letter of Recommendation
Written by Current or Former Coworker (Pharmacist)

MICHAEL JAMES HALE

555-555-5555 | Street Address, City, State, Zip | michaeljames@emailaddress.com

(Date)

Mr. (Ms.) _____
Title
(Company)
(Address 1)
(Address 2)

Dear Mr. (Ms.) _____:

I am writing you on behalf of Tonya Jones, to recommend her for your Pharmacist position at your new location in Atlanta, Georgia. Tonya and I have served as the two main Pharmacists for our current location for five years. She is looking to relocate due to her husband's career, and I know she would prove invaluable to your clientele.

Tonya is a knowledgeable pharmacist who displays a high level of customer service to our diverse customer-base. She is very familiar with the medicines prescribed to senior patients as we have a large retirement community nearby. Tonya is also highly skilled at addressing questions for parents of school age children and regularly volunteers to administer required immunizations to local students.

Tonya managed our inventory levels, ensuring we were well stocked on all needed medications and supplies. Together we regularly monitored inventory and accounted for any loss we encountered. I have been told our stockroom was the best maintained in the company, with zero infractions for controlled substances.

You will find Tonya friendly and willing to help patients get needed medicines even when issues arise with their insurance providers and/or doctor's offices. Our Rx numbers has actually increased significantly over the last five years, and I believe that is based in part on how much our customers like Tonya.

I encourage you to consider her for your new store and will be happy to answer any questions you might have in this regards. Please feel free to contact me at the above phone number or email. Thank you for your time.

Sincerely,

Michael James Hale

Professional Letter of Recommendation
Written by Current or Former Coworker (Sales Representative)

NICOLE M. ROBERTS

555-555-5555 | Street Address, City, State, Zip | nmroberts@emailaddress.com

(Date)

Mr. (Ms.) _____
Title
(Company)
(Address 1)
(Address 2)

Dear Mr. (Ms.) _____:

Patrick O'Malley has requested that I write to you to recommend him for your open sales position, and I am happy to do so. Patrick and I have worked together selling products and services for East Coast Software for two years now. I admire his tenacious efforts to generate leads and close sales with a wide-array of clients, including those who turned down other sales representatives.

Our team objectives have consistently increased every quarter for the last two years, and Patrick has been a key part of making sure we exceed those goals. He is the highest grossing member of our team, and we collectively rank as the second highest revenue generators nationwide.

Patrick excels at his job because of his excellent service and commitment to customer satisfaction. In the last six months, 20 percent of his sales came from referral business. Our manager asked him to lead training sessions to help other sales representatives to maximize their efforts and we realized a 5 percent increase the following quarter.

Patrick is energetic, hard-working, and has expressed a strong interest in selling for your company. I believe he will make an immediate and lasting impact on your sales performance and encourage you to fully consider his application. I appreciate the time you have taken to read this letter. If I can be of any additional assistance, please contact me at the phone number of email address listed above.

Sincerely,

Nicole M. Roberts

Professional Letter of Recommendation
Written by Current or Former Coworker (Registered Nurse)

ASHLEY WILLIAMS

555-555-5555 | awilliams@emailaddress.com

(Date)

Mr. (Ms.) _____
Title
(Company)
(Address 1)
(Address 2)

Dear Mr. (Ms.) _____:

Letter of Recommendation for Matthew Long

I am pleased to write to you on behalf of Matthew Long, recommending him as a Registered Nurse at your hospital. Matthew and I have worked at the same nursing home for the last three years while he completed his Bachelor's of Nursing Degree at State University. I know he has a great interest in working with patients in a hospital environment and will prove a valuable member of your team.

Having worked with Matthew on day, night, and swing shifts, I can tell you he adjusts well to changing schedules and is always kind, courteous, and respectful to his patients and their families. He excels in helping patients and family members understand their changing medical needs while trying to create the most positive visiting experiences he can for patients regardless of their age and medical situations.

Matthew is meticulous when it comes to paperwork, charts, and other patient documentation. I have worked with him on auditing patient files and was impressed with his thoroughness. Additionally, he always goes the extra mile to make sure patients have flowers or balloons or a card on their birthdays and other special occasions.

I understand that the hospital environment can be very different than our long-term care facility, but I believe Matthew will excel as part of your team. I strongly endorse his candidacy and will be happy to answer any additional questions you might have regarding his work. Please feel free to contact me at the contact information listed above. Thank you for your time.

Sincerely,

Ashley Williams

Professional Letter of Recommendation
Written by Current or Former Coworker (Payroll/Billing Specialist)

PATRICIA ROBINSON

555-555-5555 | Street Address, City, State, Zip | probinson@emailaddress.com

(Date)

Mr. (Ms.) _____
Title
(Company)
(Address 1)
(Address 2)

Dear Mr. (Ms.) _____:

Charles Williams has asked me to contact you on his behalf to recommend him as your payroll and billing specialist. I have worked with Charles in the accounting department of ABC Corp. since 2011.

Charles expertly processes payroll for 150 salaried, full-time, and part-time employees while handling billing for our major corporate clients. I partner with Charles on billing efforts, handling all of our small- to mid-level clients. Together we reduced our aged receivables 30 percent over the past year and dramatically improved our company's cash flow as a result.

I was notably impressed when Charles represented our department for IT's implementation of new financial management/accounting software. He ensured they incorporated everything we needed into the new system and that there was no interruption to payroll or billing.

On a personal level, Charles organized our company's Toys-4-Tots efforts and encouraged us all to sponsor his charity efforts for Walk for a Cure last year.

I believe he will prove himself an instant asset due to his detailed, accurate work as well as his efforts to create a positive work environment. I appreciate the time you have taken to read this letter. If I can provide any additional information to help you review Charles's candidacy, please feel free to call me at 555-555-5555 or email me at probinson@emailaddress.com.

Sincerely,

Patricia Robinson

Professional Letter of Recommendation
Written by Current or Former Coworker (Science Teacher)

PAUL DANIEL WILLIAMS, JR.

555-555-5555 | Street Address, City, State, Zip | pdwilliams1975@emailaddress.com

(Date)

Mr. (Ms.) _____
Title
(Company)
(Address 1)
(Address 2)

Dear Mr. (Ms.) _____:

I am pleased to write to you on behalf of Eileen Wright, recommending her for your open role of Biology Teacher at ABC High School. I have been working with Eileen for four years at XYZ High School in Lake County, Florida. She teaches our biology, Biology Honors, and Marine Biology courses, with average class size of 30 students per course.

Eileen handles a full course load with maximum students signed up for her classes. In addition to her work load, she serves on several committees and coaches the girls' track team. She has the energy of a 20 year old, and I am often amazed at how much she gets done in day!

Furthermore, I have heard nothing but positive things from parents regarding Eileen's work with their children. Eileen often offers tutoring sessions when students struggle with a new scientific concept, and she is very hands-on with laboratory work. I know several parents have expressed their gratitude with her effort to help their students excel in science where they had always struggled in the past.

It has been a pleasure to work with Eileen, and our department and students will miss her a great deal. However, Eileen's husband received a promotion and transfer to Texas so we understand we have to lose her. I believe our loss will be your gain, and she will make an excellent member of your faculty. If you have any additional questions, please call or email me at the contact information above.

Sincerely,

Paul Daniel Williams, Jr.

Professional Letter of Recommendation
Written by Current or Former Coworker (Veterinarian Tech)

JANICE MARIE WEBB

555-555-5555 | Street Address, City, State, Zip | jmwebb@emailaddress.com

(Date)

Mr. (Ms.) _____
Title
(Company)
(Address 1)
(Address 2)

Dear Mr. (Ms.) _____:

Letter of Recommendation for Suzan Longfellow

I am writing to you today on behalf of Suzan Longfellow who tells me she
is interested in the veterinarian technician position at your animal hospital.
I have been working with Suzan for several months at Home Retailer Store
while she completed her training and licensing course work at Vocational
Tech School.

Suzan is already a highly rated cashier in the store and provides excellent
customer service to all of our clientele, even the hard to please customers.
She is friendly, respectful, and knowledgeable, often answering questions
about products and services that other cashiers would be unable to address.
However, as good of an employee as Suzan is, I know her passion is to work
with animals.

I believe you will find Suzan a quick learner with a really strong work ethic.
She will also do everything she can to make your patients and their pets feel
comfortable and safe in your clinic. Having recently lost her 17-year old cat,

Suzan knows and respects what owners go through at times of grief with their pets, and I believe her sensitivity will win you long-term customer loyalty.

I strongly recommend Suzan for this position and encourage you to call me if I can be of any further assistance in her consideration. Thank you for your time.

Sincerely,

Janice Marie Webb

Professional Letter of Recommendation
Written by Current or Former Coworker (Technical Team Lead)

ASHLEY M. ANDREWS

555-555-5555 | Street Address, City, State, Zip | ama1980@emailaddress.com

(Date)

Mr. (Ms.) _____
Title
(Company)
(Address 1)
(Address 2)

Dear Mr. (Ms.) _____:

Jason Thomas asked me to contact you on his behalf to recommend him for the role of Technician Team Leader, and I am very pleased to do so. Jason has been working in the areas of wireless, telecom, and networks for more than ten years, five of which we worked for the same company. He is very knowledgeable in building infrastructure and networks, maintaining network/server performance, and upgrading technology tools as needed.

I've worked with Jason on numerous projects over the last five years, including a transition to Cisco routers, switchers, and servers. We also completed an infrastructure revamp that improved performance 25 percent. Jason regularly commits to providing 24/7 technical support to help some of our employees with more family obligations. At this point, Jason is simply looking for roles with greater scope and accountability than we can provide, but I strongly endorse him for your company.

When it comes to credentials, I know Jason has several Cisco and tool certifications. He is also highly adept at Agile and SDLC methodologies. Jason is not just knowledgeable on technical tools and applications, but also affective at translating that expertise in project oversight for major clients. Additionally, he offers some success in managing team members and budgets.

I strongly endorse Jason's application for your technical team and believe you will benefit from his presence. I appreciate the time you have taken to read this letter. If you have any questions, please just contact me at the phone or email address above.

Sincerely,

Ashley M. Andrews

Professional Letter of Recommendation
Written by Current or Former Coworker (IT Manager)

CHERYL MATTHEWS

555-555-5555 | Street Address, City, State, Zip | cmatthews123@emailaddress.com

(Date)

Mr. (Ms.) _____
Title
(Company)
(Address 1)
(Address 2)

Dear Mr. (Ms.) _____:

Sarah Miller asked me to contact you to recommend her for the role of IT Manager, and I am very pleased to do so. Sarah worked with me at our former employer, ABC Consultants, where I managed her in providing clients with wireless, telecom, and network solutions for more than five years.

Sarah delivers exceptional customer service and ensures all of her assignments are completed on-time and to full client satisfaction. Examples of her achievements/competencies include:

- Strong work ethic, providing hands-on leadership on all aspects of projects from requirements gathering and planning to user acceptance and training.

- Effective manager, hiring and developing contractors who could be used on repeated assignments and counted on to deliver high quality work product.

- Contributes to client acquisition and gains business through customer referrals.

After I left ABC Consultants, I understand Sarah started her own consulting business to give herself more flexibility while her children were young. We share some mutual business associates, and I have always heard excellent things about her as an IT expert and businesswoman.

I strongly endorse Sarah's application for your IT Manager role and believe you will benefit greatly from her leadership. I appreciate the time you have taken to read this letter. If you have any questions, please just contact me at the phone or email address above.

Sincerely,

Cheryl Matthews

Professional Letter of Recommendation
Written by Current or Former Work Associate (Management)

WILLIAM DRUM

555-555-5555 | Street Address, City, State, Zip | williamdrum@emailaddress.com

(Date)

Mr. (Ms.) _____
(Company)
(Address 1)
(Address 2)

Dear Mr. (Ms.) _____:

I am writing you on behalf of Charles Compton, who has asked me to serve as a reference for him. Mr. Compton works for me at WidgetsRUs, and I have had the opportunity to partner with him on many assignments. Charles has told me of his desire to advance to a higher position with your company and I highly endorse his application with you.

Mr. Compton has an excellent work ethic and response time, regularly going above and beyond the duties of his position. It is not uncommon for me to see him at work late or early, resolving some issue that others might have put off. Please consider these examples of his work:

- He proposed process changes that when implemented saved the company $17K per year.
- He provides dynamic and enthusiastic product demonstrations that help our sales team land key strategic clients.
- He delivers training sessions for employees and users that ensure they maximize the benefit of our product features.

Having demonstrated commitment and passion for his work and solid leadership abilities, I believe Mr. Compton is a natural choice for a senior management position and I support his efforts. I am confident he would be as much of an asset to your organization as he has been to WidgetsRUs.

I appreciate the time you took to read this letter and I will happily answer any additional questions you might have as you review his application. You can reach me at 555-555-5555 or at the email listed above. Thank you and have a wonderful day.

Sincerely,

William Drum
Title

Professional Letter of Recommendation
Written by Current or Former Employer (Sales Manager)

SARAH MARCH

555-555-5555 | Street Address, City, State, Zip | sarahmarch@emailaddress.com

(Date)

Mr. (Ms.) _____
Title
(Company)
(Address 1)
(Address 2)

Dear Mr. (Ms.) _____:

Letter of Recommendation for John Smith

John Smith has asked me to write to you recommending his work as a Regional Sales Manager for my company, Women's Products, Inc. It is my pleasure to give him the highest recommendation for his customer service, sales production, and team leadership skills.

I hired John as a Sales Associate ten years ago and quickly promoted him to Manager and then Regional Manager because of his ability to generate top sales figures and mentor his team members to do the same. John has a talent for learning product features and benefits quickly and communicating value to consumers in such a way as to quickly win buy-in and encourage long-term customer loyalty.

John led several successful product launches, each time surpassing our projected sales goals for the region. He is a popular manager because of his commitment to working with each direct report to help them understand their audience and customize their sales strategies so they can reach and surpass their revenue targets.

Over the last seven years, John has enjoyed traveling for work and was the top rated sales manager in my company. Now that he and his wife are expecting their second child and they want to live closer to her ailing parents, John has decided to look outside my organization for work so that he can settle in Dallas and focus his time in the Dallas/Fort Worth area.

While my team will miss John, I can assure you that my loss would be your gain, and he will quickly prove to be a valuable member of your team. If I can be of any additional assistance as you consider Jacob's candidacy, please feel free to contact me at the phone or email address listed above.

Sincerely,

Sarah March
Title

Professional Letter of Recommendation
Written by Current or Former Employer (Operations Manager)

JAMES ANDERSON

555-555-5555 | Street address, city, state, zip | jamesanderson@emailaddress.Com

(Date)

Mr. (Ms.) _____
Title
(Company)
(Address 1)
(Address 2)

Dear Mr. (Ms.) _____:

I am writing you on behalf of Michelle Jones, who has asked me to serve as a reference for her for your open position of operations manager. Ms. Jones has managed our production operations at XYZ Products, Inc., for several years with the scope of her leadership ranging from facility management to manufacturing and warehouse management.

I was disappointed to learn that Ms. Jones will be relocating with her husband, and I am sorry to lose her here at XYX Products. Please allow me to provide you with a brief glimpse of her work with us:

- Managed a warehouse with $30M inventory while installing automation and new technologies to enhance efficiency and create a $10K per year cost savings.

- Coordinated effectively with clients, from Fortune 500 clients to small businesses, ensuring production was capable of meeting quality and volume requirements.

- Served as go-to person to turnaround delayed or troubled projects, adjusting for obstacles and last minute changes to ensure on-time project delivery and full customer satisfaction.

While my team will miss Michelle, I can assure you that my loss would be your gain, and she will quickly prove to be a valuable member of your team. If I can be of any additional assistance as you consider Michelle's candidacy, please feel free to contact me at the phone or email address listed above.

Sincerely,

James Anderson
Title

Professional Letter of Recommendation
Written by Current or Former Employer (E-Marketing Manager)

ALICE SMITH

555-555-5555 | Street Address, City, State, Zip | alicesmith@emailaddress.com

(Date)

Mr. (Ms.) _____
Title
(Company)
(Address 1)
(Address 2)

Dear Mr. (Ms.) _____:

I am writing you today regarding Stacey Jones' candidacy for your marketing manager position. Stacey worked for me in my previous role at as Vice President of Sales & Marketing for XYZ Inc., and I am pleased to recommend her for your company now.

During the time I worked at XYZ Inc., we initiated several digital marketing strategies that I entrusted to Stacey. Her creativity and understanding of e-Marketing strategies and search engine optimization needs allowed us establish a strong web presence and shape social media campaigns that reached a whole new demographic for us. Stacey spent considerable time working with our IT department to make sure we had an interactive website that was highly user friendly.

Stacey was not just a creative force in the marketing department; she also has a keen understanding of business goals and bottom-lines. Stacey's work was not only highly effective, but demonstrated strong return on investment. She achieved these results in part by championing advancements in our e-Commerce capabilities so that when customers found us online, they could also securely purchase products at the same time.

When I was persuaded by a friend to help lead a startup operation with him, I asked Stacey to join us, but as a new mother, she was not seeking a new role at that point in time. She has told me now that her children are older and she has completed her MBA that she wants a more advanced leadership role and there is little room for advancement at our old company.

For these reasons, I believe she would be a strong asset for your operation. I would hire her myself, but I cannot offer her the opportunities your company can. I strongly endorse Stacey's application with you, and I believe you will quickly consider her as valuable an asset as I did. If I can answer any additional questions, please contact me at the number or email address listed above. Thank you for your time and consideration.

Sincerely,

Alice Smith
Title

Professional Letter of Recommendation
Written by Current or Former Employer (Office Administrator)

FRANK ROBINSON

Phone | Street Address, City, State, Zip | email address

(Date)

Mr. (Ms.) _____
(Company)

(Address 1)
(Address 2)

Dear Mr. (Ms.) _____:

I am writing to you today on behalf of Michelle Smith, who has asked me to endorse her application to be your new Office Manager. Michelle worked for me last summer as an intern and did an exceptional job; I am very pleased to recommend her to you. I found Michelle to be organized, to complete tasks promptly and effectively, and to be a fast problem solver.

My office is comprised of four lawyers, each handling a different practice area. Michelle was our back-up Office Administrator for the summer while our main employee was returning from maternity leave and settling back in. It was a very helpful and productive internship for our office and for Michelle. She made travel arrangements for our lawyers as needed, maintained their court schedules, and proofed and managed communications between lawyers and clients and lawyers and the courts.

Ms. Smith also spent the summer handling the purchasing of office supplies and working with our vendors to ensure the staff was fully equipped for whatever needs they had. After a month of proving herself, I also trusted her to handle some financial bookkeeping in cooperation with our accountant.

While I do not have room for her at my office at the moment, I would definitely hire Michelle myself if I did and I strongly recommend her for your open position. I appreciate your time in reading this letter and if you need to reach me for any additional questions, please feel free to call or email me at the contact information above.

Sincerely,

Frank Robinson
Title

Professional Letter of Recommendation (Sales) – Email Format

To: michaelthomas@email.com
From: sharonjones@email.com
Subject: George Short's Application

Dear Mr. Thomas,

I am pleased to write to you on behalf of George Short, recommending him for your position of Regional Sales Manager. Prior to my personal promotion to Vice President of Sales, I managed George as our East Coast Sales Director and I found him to be an excellent leader and revenue producer. Allow me to summarize some of his contributions:

* Consistently surpassed sales goals by as much as 30%, driving team revenue of $10M+ per year.
* Mentored three sales associates to promotions as sales managers and ensured a staff of more than 20 met or exceeded their personal sales goals.
* Launched four products in competitive markets to achieve projected revenue goals in the region.
* Won multiple awards for benchmark achievements and was rated as a superior manager by his team.

Outside of work, George places a strong emphasis on community service and regularly organized employee participation in charity events. He excelled in creating strong corporate ties to the community and positive public perception.

I regret that we are reorganizing the company and condensing our team. While I would have kept George as part of our team, he volunteered to look for new opportunities to provide other employees job security. I believe George will prove to be a valuable member of your team and encourage you to contact me if you have any additional questions. Thank you for your time and consideration.

Sincerely,

Sharon Jones
555-555-5555
sharonjones@email.com

Professional Letter of Recommendation (Operations Manager) – Email Format

To: GeorgeJonesCEO@email.com
From: rebeccalharris@email.com
Subject: Shane Taylor

Dear George Jones,

I am pleased to write to you on behalf of Shane Taylor, recommending him for your open position of Operations Manager. I have worked with Shane at Widgets-R-Us for five years and can attest to his ability to effectively run a production floor in a manufacturing environment. My job has been to oversee the safety and environmental compliance functions of our operation and Shane always supported my efforts.

While I worked to achieve and maintain ISO certifications, Shane organized training sessions to ensure our new policies and procedures were understood and adhered to by more than 100 production floor workers, over three shifts. Despite stricter regulations, Shane was able to increase his production numbers and quality ratings during the same period.

As a manager, Shane is a well-respected, hands-on leader who arrives early and leaves late. I believe Shane will make an immediate, positive difference in your organization, and I highly endorse his application. If I can answer any additional questions about Shane's work, please feel free to call me on my cell at 555-555-5555 or email me on my personal account at beckyr@email.com. Thank you for your time.

Best Regards,

Rebecca L. Harris
555-555-5555
rebeccalharris@email.com

Professional Letter of Recommendation
(IT Team Leader) – Email Format

To: MichaelJones@email.com
From: CMWilliams@email.com
Subject: Sidney Jones

Dear Michael,

Sidney Jones requested that I write to you on his behalf, recommending him for your open position of IT Team Leader. I have been working with Sidney for the past year on a software development project for Major Financial Client. When Sidney joined the team, he was not the official leader, but he did take the lead in turning around our lagging, over budget project.

Our assignment has changed project managers three times since its inception, and this created a sense of discontinuity and a software program that was not meeting the needs of our client's end-users. Sidney came on the project and brought us together to identify where were we missing the user requirements and formulate a plan to correct the issues. Without any special pay or recognition, Sidney got us back on track and we delivered the program this month to a very pleased client.

I would describe Sidney as a hard-working, innovative, cost-conscious problem solver. Aside from working on our project, Sidney helped identify areas where our team and other department personnel could benefit from additional training. He successfully organized training sessions for employees to complete certifications, including instruction on Agile development methods.

I believe you would benefit from Sidney's technical and leadership expertise and highly recommend him for your company. I appreciate the time you have spent reading this letter. If you need any additional information regarding Sidney, please feel free to contact me at the phone or email listed above.

Sincerely,

Christopher M. Williams
555-555-5555
CMWilliams@email.com

Professional Letter of Recommendation (Pharmacist) – Email Format

To: CrystalWhite@email.com
From: MichaelJHale@email.com
Subject: Tonya Jones' Application

Dear Crystal,

I am writing you on behalf of Tonya Jones to recommend her for your Pharmacist position at your new location in Atlanta, Georgia. Tonya and I have served as the two main Pharmacists for our current location for five years. She is looking to relocate due to her husband's career and I know she would prove invaluable to your clientele.

Tonya is a knowledgeable pharmacist who displays a high level of customer service to our diverse customer-base. She is highly familiar with the medicines prescribed to senior patients as we have a large-retirement community nearby. Tonya is also highly skilled at addressing questions for parents of school aged children and regularly volunteers to administer required immunizations to local students.

You will find Tonya friendly and willing to help patients get needed medicines even when issues arose with their insurance providers and/or doctor's offices. Our Rx numbers has actually increased significantly over the last five years and I believe that is based in part on how much our customers like Tonya.

I encourage you to consider her for your new store and will be happy to answer any questions you might have in this regards. Please feel free to contact me at the above phone number or email. Thank you for your time.

Sincerely,

Michael James Hale
555-555-5555
MichaelJHale@email.com

Professional Letter of Recommendation (Sales Representative) – Email Format

To: AMJones@email.com
From: NicoleRoberts@email.com
Subject: Patrick O'Malley's Application

Dear Amanda,

Patrick O'Malley has requested that I write to you to recommend him for your open sales position and I am happy to do so. Patrick and I have worked together selling products and services for East Coast Software for two years now. I admire his tenacious efforts to generate leads and close sales with a wide-array of clients, including those that turned down other sales representatives.

Our team objectives have consistently increased every quarter for the last two years and Patrick has been a key part of making sure we exceed those goals. His is the highest grossing member of our team, and we collectively rank as the second highest revenue generators nationwide.

Patrick excels at his job because of his excellent service and commitment to customer satisfaction. In the last six months, 20 percent of his sales came from referral business. Our manager asked him to lead training sessions to help other sales representatives to maximize their efforts and we realized a 5 percent increase the following quarter.

Patrick is energetic, hard-working, and has expressed a strong interest in selling for your company. I believe he will make an immediate and lasting impact on your sales performance and encourage you to fully consider his application. I appreciate the time you have taken to read this letter. If I can be of any additional assistance, please contact me at the phone number and email in my signature.

Sincerely,

Nicole M. Roberts
555-555-5555
NicoleRoberts@email.com

Professional Letter of Recommendation (Registered Nurse) – Email Format

To: kjw123@email.com
From: AGWilliams@email.com
Subject: Matthew Long

Dear Kimberly White,

I am pleased to write to you on behalf of Matthew Long, recommending his application as a registered nurse at your hospital. Matthew and I have worked at the same nursing home for the last three years while he completed his Bachelor's of Nursing Degree at State University. I know he has a great interest in working with patients in a hospital environment and will prove a valuable member of your team.

Having worked with Matthew on day, night, and swing shifts, I can tell you he adjusts well to changing schedules and is always kind, courteous, and respectful to his patients and their families. He excels in helping patients and family members understand their changing medical needs while trying to create the most positive visiting experiences he can for patients regardless of their age and medical situations.

I understand that the hospital environment can be very different than our long-term care facility, but I believe Matthew will excel as part of your team. I strongly endorse his candidacy and will be happy to answer any additional questions you might have regarding his work. Please feel free to contact me at the contact information listed below. Thank you for your time.

Sincerely,

Ashley Williams
555-555-5555
AGWilliams@email.com

Professional Letter of Recommendation (Payroll/Billing Specialist) – Email Format

To: jcs123@email.com
From: probinson@emailaddress.com
Subject: Charles Williams' Application

Dear Julian,

Charles Williams has asked me to contact you on his behalf to recommend his application as your payroll and billing specialist. I have worked with Charles in the accounting department of ABC Corp. since 2011. Please consider the following:

* Charles processes payroll for 150 salaried, full-time, and part-time employees while handling billing for our major corporate clients.

* Charles reduced aged receivables 30 percent over the past year and dramatically improved our company's cash flow as a result.

* He represented our department for IT's implementation of new financial management/accounting software and ensured they incorporated everything we needed into the new system and that there was no interruption to payroll or billing.

I believe he will prove himself an instance asset due to his detailed, accurate work as well as his efforts to create a positive work environment. I appreciate the time you have taken to read this letter. If I can provide any additional information to help you review Charles's candidacy, please feel free to call me at 555-555-5555 or email me at probinson@emailaddress.com.

Sincerely,

Patricia Robinson
probinson@emailaddress.com

Professional Letter of Recommendation (Science Teacher) – Email Format

To: gatormanager@companyname.com
From: pdwilliams@email.com
Subject: Eileen Wright's Application

Dear Steven,

I am pleased to write to you on behalf of Eileen Wright, recommending her for your open role of Biology Teacher at ABC High School. I have been working with Eileen for four years at XYZ High School in Lake County, Florida. She teaches our biology, biology honors, and marine biology courses, with average class size of 30 students per course.

Eileen handles a full course load with maximum students signed up for her classes. In addition to her work load, she serves on several committees and coaches the girl's track team. She has the energy of a 20 year old and I am often amazed at how much she gets done in day! Furthermore, I have heard nothing but positive things from parents regarding Eileen's work with their children.

It has been a pleasure to work with Eileen and our department and students will miss her a great deal. However, Eileen's husband received a promotion and transfer to Texas, so we understand we have to lose her. I believe our loss will be your gain and she will make an excellent member of your faculty. If you have any additional questions, please call or email me at the contact information above.

Sincerely,

Paul Daniel Williams, Jr.
Science Department Head, ABC High School
pdwilliams@email.com
555-555-5555

Professional Letter of Recommendation (Veterinarian Tech) – Email Format

To: TrishRoberts@email.com
From: janicemariewebb@email.com
Subject: Suzan Longfellow's Application

Dear Trish,

I am writing to you today on behalf of Suzan Longfellow who tells me she is interested in the veterinarian technician position at your animal hospital. I have been working with Suzan for several months at Home Retailer Store while she completed her training and licensing course work at Vocational Tech School.

Suzan is already a highly rated cashier in the store and provides excellent customer service to all of our clientele, even the hard to please customers. She is friendly, respectful, and knowledgeable, often answering questions about products and services that other cashiers would be unable to address. However, as good of an employee as Suzan is, I know her passion is to work with animals.

I believe you will find Suzan a quick learner with really strong work ethic. She will also do everything she can to make your patients and their pets feel comfortable and safe in your clinic. I strongly recommend Suzan for this position and encourage you to call me if I can be of any further assistance in her consideration. Thank you for your time.

Sincerely,

Janice Marie Webb
555-555-5555

Professional Letter of Recommendation (Technical Team Lead) – Email Format

To: susanlittle@email.com
From: ashleyandrews@email.com
Subject: Jason Thomas' Application

Dear Susan Little,

Jason Thomas asked me to contact you on his behalf to recommend him for the role of Technician Team Leader and I am very pleased to do so. Jason has been working in the areas of wireless, telecom, and networks for more than ten years (five of which we worked for the same company). He is very knowledgeable in building infrastructure and networks, maintaining network/server performance, and upgrading technology tools as needed.

I've worked with Jason on numerous projects over the last five years, including a transition to Cisco routers, switchers, and servers. We also completed an infrastructure revamp that improved performance 25 percent. Jason regularly commits to providing 24/7 technical support to help some of our employees with more family obligations. When it comes to credentials, I know Jason has several Cisco and tool certifications. He is also highly adept at Agile and SDLC methodologies.

I strongly endorse Jason's application for you technical team and believe you will benefit for his presence. I appreciate the time you have taken to read this letter. If you have any questions, please just contact me at the phone or email address above.

Sincerely,

Ashley M. Andrews
555-555-5555
ashleyandrews@email.com

Professional Letter of Recommendation
(IT Manager) – Email Format

To: AshleyJThomas@email.com
From: CJMatthews@email.com
Subject: Sarah Miller's Application

Dear Ashley,

Sarah Miller asked me to contact you to recommend her for the role of IT Manager and I am very pleased to do so. Sarah worked with me at our former employer, ABC Consultants, where I managed her in providing clients with wireless, telecom, and network solutions for more than five years.

As you review her application, please consider the following:

* Sarah possesses a strong work ethic, providing hands-on leadership on all aspects of projects from requirements gathering and planning to user acceptance and training.

* She is an effective manager, hiring and developing contractors who could be used on repeated assignments and counted on to deliver high quality work product.

* Sarah contributes to client acquisition and gains business through customer referrals.

After I left ABC Consultants, I understand Sarah started her own consulting business to give herself more flexibility while her children were young. We share some mutual business associates, and I have always heard excellent things about her as an IT expert and business woman. I strongly endorse Sarah's application for your IT Manager role and if you have any questions, please just contact me at the phone number below.

Sincerely,

Cheryl Matthews
555-555-5555

Professional Letter of Recommendation (Accounting Director) – Email Format

To: JasonRobinson@email.com
From: jsmith@widgetsdirect.com
Subject: William Jones' Application

Dear Jason Robinson,

I am pleased to write this letter on behalf of William Jones, who worked with me in the financial department of Widgets Direct. As the CFO of an early stage company, I relied on my accounting director, William, immensely to ensure our domestic and international sales growth was fully compliant with all applicable regulations and tax codes.

I recruited William from a Big 4 Accounting agency and was very pleased with his contributions. His consultancy work parleyed into expert advice for us that helped us establish a business presence in 12 countries across Europe and Asia while doubling our revenue performance in the US.

As a manager, William recruited a solid team and took an interest in their professional development. Two of his staff earned their CPA licenses under his mentorship. William regularly led training sessions on financial management, tax code, and proper software utilization. The staff he recruited, developed, and mentored is still in tack and performing very well.

I highly recommend William for your open position and encourage you to consider him a valuable business partner. I can assure you that he will help you realize whatever growth objectives you have for your company while infusing your accounting/finance department with the highest levels of professional standards. If I can provide any additional information for your consideration of William's candidacy, please let me know.

Sincerely,

John Smith
Chief Financial Officer
jsmith@widgetsdirect.com
555-555-5555

Professional Letter of Recommendation (Finance Director) – Email Format

To: AJHale@email.com
From: lisajones@acmexyz.com
Subject: Bethany Smith

Dear Andrew,

I am pleased to write this letter on behalf of Bethany Smith, who has been a vital member of my financial team at Acme XYZ for seven years. During this time, I have relied on her to ensure our US and international sales growth was achieved in full compliance with all applicable regulations and that our accounting functions were completed accurately and completely each year.

Highlights of her work include the following:

* Developed strategies for successful market penetration in South America and Eastern Europe.
* Hired and mentored financial and accounting managers to facilitate international growth.
* Enhanced profit margins 10 percent as the company increased revenue 25 percent.
* Fostered a collaborative work environment and highly engaged workforce.

When Bethany told me that her husband had been promoted and transferred out West, I knew I was losing a team member that would be incredibly hard to replace. I highly recommend Bethany for your open position of Finance Director and will be happy to provide you any additional information you might need. Thank you for your time today.

Sincerely,

Lisa Jones
Chief Executive Officer
555-555-5555
lisajones@acmexyz.com

Professional Letter of Recommendation (Software Engineer) – Email Format

To: athonywilliams@email.com
From: jbgood@emailaddress.com
Subject: Michael Thomas

Dear Anthony Williams,

I am writing you to recommend Michael Thomas for the position of Software Development Engineer. I managed Michael in my former role as Vice President of Product Development for Major IT Company, Inc., I would like to provide you with a brief overview of Michael's work – please consider:

* Michael worked on developing five major releases and dozens of software updates. He managed the software development life cycle for his assigned products, which upon release realized millions of dollars in revenue.
* Michael's work spanned several product areas, including financial management, banking, scheduling/calendar organization, and graphic design.
* Michael proved himself a quick learner and easily adapted when our company transitioned to Agile methodologies. He also quickly gained his certification through IEEE.

I believe Major IT Company benefited from Michael's employment and you will as well. If I can answer any additional questions about his qualifications, expertise, or achievements, I will be happy to do so.

Sincerely,

Jack B. Good
Title
555-555-5555
jbgood@emailaddress.com

Professional Letter of Recommendation (HR Generalist) – Email Format

To: RobertLangley@email.com
From: JamesAtkins@email.com
Subject: Janice Langston

Dear Robert,

Janice Langston has asked me to recommend her for your open position of Human Resources Generalist and it my pleasure to do so. Janice has been working for my company for ten years, covering the dual role of HR Manager and Office Administrator. Now that I am look at retirement, I will be selling the company and Janice is looking for a new opportunity.

When I hired Janice, she was working on her Bachelor's in Human Resources Management with the University of Florida. Since that time, she has completed her education and made several contributions, including:

* She worked with me while my company acquired a competitor and experienced 150 percent growth.
* She worked on analyzing and selecting benefits plans for our employees and communicating the details of those plans, and any relevant changes, to our staff.
* She has also recommended and implemented two upgrades to our personnel and payroll management systems. As a result, she is highly qualified in applications such as QuickBooks and PeopleSoft.

As the office administrator, Janice professionally handled employee, client, and vendor communications and managed office staff personnel. I highly recommend her for your Human Resources Generalist role and will happily provide any additional information if you need it. Thank you for your time and consideration.

Sincerely,

James Atkins
555-555-5555
JamesAtkins@email.com

Professional Letter of Recommendation (Sales Manager) – Email Format (Personal)

To: sigsoto@email.com
From: jasmith@email.com
Subject: Ayla Jones

Dear Sigmarie,

Hi there! I hope everything is going well with your new product launch. I wanted to connect with you today regarding my former employee, Ayla Jones, who has asked me to serve as a reference on her behalf. She is relocating to the state of Florida in just two weeks and is interested in your Sales Director position in the state.

I would like to provide you with a couple of quick notes regarding her work:

* Ayla is an energetic sales professional and will bring a passion for promoting your product that extends beyond a desire to make quota or commission.
* Ayla consistently exceeded her sales targets and was a pivotal part of making sure my store was rated highest in the nation for revenue dollars, customer service, and client retention.
* Ayla had a talent for pairing products to customer wants and budgets and I received several letters notes from pleased customers in regards to her extra efforts.

Since our time working together, Ayla earned an MBA and held two management positions. Even when she was working for me, I could see she had a talent for managing and training staff. I highly recommend Ayla for your open position. If I can provide any additional information, please call or email me.

Best regards,

Jessica Anne Smith
Title
555-555-5555
jasmith@email.com

Professional Letter of Recommendation
(Logistics Supervisor) – Email Format (Personal)

To: probinson@emailaddress.com
From: jjsmith123@emailaddress.com
Subject: Timothy Jones

Dear Patrick,

Hi there! I hope everything is going well with your kids' soccer game last week – it was so great to see you at the planning session for the upcoming regional meet. I wanted to touch base with you today to provide a short recommendation for Timothy Jones who is applying for the Logistics Supervisor opening.

I believe Timothy has already met with your Human Resources Director, and I just wanted to provide him with my additional endorsements and encourage you to meet with him directly. Please consider the following:

*   Timothy was hired as a Supply Chain Specialist to plan delivery routes for chemical products via land, air, and sea. He is also trained on OSHA requirements and ensured full regulatory compliance for all delivery efforts.
*   Timothy was promoted to Warehouse Supervisor and most recently to Warehouse Manager to oversee the processing and storage of tens of thousands of products daily with collective value in the seven-figure range.
*   Timothy is a solid recruiter, trainer, and union liaison and is highly rated by his peers and direct reports.

While I would love to keep Timothy in-house, he has expressed a strong interest in moving closer to his parents. Your logistics office in Georgia would be an ideal fit for him and I believe he will prove a strong asset for your company. I appreciate the time you have spent reading this letter. If I can provide any additional information while you consider Timothy's application, please contact me at the contact information listed above.

Sincerely,

Jillian Jones Smith
Title
jjsmith123@emailaddress.com
555-555-5555

Professional Letter of Recommendation (Graphic Designer) – Email Format (Personal)

To: dljohnson@email.com
From: andrewrjohnson@email.com
Subject: Mary Shueller

Dear Duane,

Hi there! I just wanted to drop you a quick note about my friend and former employee, Mary Shueller. I believe she has already applied for your open role of Graphics Designer and you are scheduled to meet with her personally next week. I believe you will find her to be a creative and energetic professional with a keen eye for translating written messages into visual communication.

I'm sure Mary will bring her portfolio with her to show you, and I want to tell you a little about my work with her and some of the things you might see. When I was Marketing Manager with XYZ Corporation, I entrusted Mary with creating a wide-range of print and digital pieces for customer communications.

Having worked on MAC computers since she was a child, Mary added several MACs to our office and implemented the latest upgrade of Adobe Creative Suites. She trained most of our creative team on both the new computers and software programs.

In addition to her print work, Mary made several contributions to our web page and social media pages. In one instance, she designed a facebook ad that garnered tens of thousands of hits and increased our website orders 10%.

As you know, I left XYZ Corporation in 2010 to take a more executive role with a larger company, but Mary's son plays soccer with my daughter so we have kept in touch. From a professional and personal point of view, I believe she will be a great asset to your team. If I can be of any additional assistance, please give me a call.

Sincerely,

Andrew R. Johnson
Title
555-555-5555
andrewrjohnson@email.com

Professional Letter of Recommendation (Restaurant Manager) – Email Format (Personal)

To: cjsmanager@email.com
From: mls@emailaddress.com
Subject: Alex Hernandez

Dear Charlene,

Hi there! It was great to see you at the community fundraiser last week for the Boy's Club. I hope everything is going well for you personally and professionally. I wanted to drop you a quick note regarding one of the applicants for Restaurant Manager for your new location in Miami, Florida. If you have time, maybe we can meet up for lunch to catch up and discuss in more detail Alex's application.

In the meantime, please allow me to endorse Alex Hernandez for this position and highlight some of his qualifications. Consider:

* Alex has worked for me as a Chef and Catering Coordinator and I find him to be an excellent judge of menu selection and pricing as well as a rock solid kitchen/event manager.
* Alex completed Bachelor's degree last year and is looking to blend his formal business management training with his hands-on experience in the restaurant world.
* Alex is highly skilled in customer service and frequently receives compliments on his work from our patrons.
* Alex is certified in food safety and trained on the most recent laws and regulations. He also keeps his team – bartenders in particular – knowledgeable of drink and dietary trends so they can answer customer questions with confidence and expertise.

I fully endorse Alex's application and would be happy to provide additional information. Please feel free to call me or email me back at your convenience. Thank you and have a great day!

Best Regards,

Michelle Lee Smith
Title
mls@emailaddress.com
555-555-5555

Professional Letter of Recommendation
(Benefits Coordinator) – Email Format (Personal)

To: sjt@email.com
From: davidlsmith@email.com
Subject: Emilio Rodriguez

Dear Sarah,

Hi there! I am writing you today on behalf of Emilio Rodriguez, to endorse his application as your new Benefits and Compensation Manager. Emilio is a long-time family friend with whom I did have a chance to work several years ago at XYZ Corporation.

At that point, Emilio proved himself to be a highly skilled human resources professional with comprehensive experience in payroll management, vendor relations, and benefits selection/administration. He also managed our sales commission program and 401 (k) plan.

Emilio oversaw compensation and commission payments for 150 sales representatives across the US and also identified those who would receive designation in the President's Club each year. This involves tracking millions of dollars in sales revenue and awarding tens of thousands of dollars in bonuses and Emilio performed this task without error.

In regards to our 401 (k) plan, Emilio selected the financial provider and ensured accurate administration for 300+ company employees. In the past, he handled our payroll function and health insurance benefits.

I believe Emilio has the necessary skills to be a valuable member of your team, and I would gladly hire him on my staff now if I had an opening. I strongly urge you to meet with him in person and get to know him a bit yourself as you consider his application. If I can be of any additional help, please give me a call.

Sincerely,

David L. Smith
Title
davidlsmith@email.com
555-555-5555

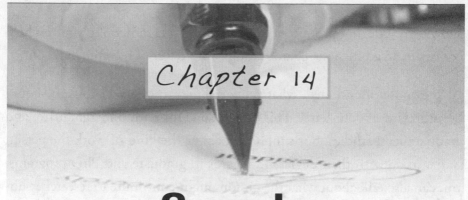

Chapter 14

Sample Academic Letters of Recommendation

Chapter 8 details some of the content and strategies that are important for academic-focused letters of recommendation. No matter what your relationship with the candidate is, you need to communicate two overall concepts: how he/she is prepared to achieve his/her academic goals and what value he/she offers a program.

Whether the candidate is applying to an undergraduate or graduate program, law school, or medical school, competition can be fierce. You might think that as long as a school gets paid, they do not care if their students excel or drop out, but that is not true. Many schools build their reputations on the success of their graduates, and if these students do not excel, the school's reputation may suffer. Thus, schools want to bring in students who show a great deal of promise academically. That is something you can help convey to an admissions board through your letter of recommendation.

As previously mentioned, what value the person offers a program should be addressed in your letter. This can be done for both undergraduate- and graduate-level studies, but simply talk about the kind of work the person wants to do with their degree. In regards to graduate and PhD programs, you can also talk about what the person might contribute to research, publications, classroom discussion, or teaching. Please review the following brainstorming questions and then look through the sample letters for how to combine them into a solid letter presentation.

Questions regarding how the person performed academically:

- What type of grades did the person earn?
- What type of work did they complete and how well did they perform?
- Does this person contribute to and/or lead group work or classroom discussions?
- Is this person on-time and respectful in class?
- Does this person assist fellow students?
- How well does this person write, test, and/or present?
- Did this person challenge themselves or take less challenging courses?

Questions regarding the character of the person:

- How well does this person manage multiple assignments/tasks?
- How well does this person prioritize between responsibilities?
- Does this person manage his/her time well?
- Does this person take on extra work or put in more effect to ensure a project is completed well?
- How does this person distinguish themselves as a student?
- Does this person deal well with change and/or challenges?

Questions relating to your relationship with the subject of the letter:

-What impresses you most about the candidate?

-What characteristics would you say describe the candidate the most?

-How have you seen the person grow or change as a student?

-How passionate is this person about their academic pursuits?

-Would you admit this person into this field of study?

You do not need to answer all of these questions in one single letter of recommendation, but you should try to answer several together as you tell stories in relation to the candidate. But please note, of all the questions, stating that you would admit the person into that field is important. It states that the person is both ready for the work and that he or she has identified the right course of study to pursue. This tells a college that it can invest in the student and expect good results.

Note to Applicants

When you are asking professors who have hundreds of students - in one class alone, sometimes - for letters of recommendation, carefully consider the relationship you had with that professor.

Dr. Shannon Bow O'Brien from the University of Texas, Austin, recalled an instance when she had a student from a large lecture session filled with nearly 200 students ask her for a letter of recommendation. When asked if they had spoken before, the student told her, "No, but I was the one who always wore that bright hat and sat in the middle."

You should note that chances are, unless you are a student who stands out, your professor is more noticeable to you than you are to him/her. For a professor to write you a solid letter, he or she needs to have some idea of who you are. Therefore, it is best to ask professors who taught you in a smaller classroom setting and with whom you interacted with on some level. Also, the more recently he or she taught you or the more frequently you had a professor for a class, the better.

Academic Letter of Recommendation from a Current or Former Employer (University Admissions)

GERALD JONES

555-555-5555 | Street Address, City, State, Zip | geraldjones123@emailaddress.com

(Date)

Mr. (Ms.) _____
Title
(Company)
(Address 1)
(Address 2)

Dear Mr. (Ms.) _____:

I am writing to you on behalf of Johann Johnson to recommend him for admission into your university. Johann works as a sales associate at the MegaBookStore I manage while pursuing his associate degree at the local community college. Johann is fully committed to his academics, but still gives his full effort.

I find him to be a clean-cut, hard-working professional with strong product knowledge and excellent customer service. Johann's schedule varies from 15 to 25 hours per week (more at the holidays), but no matter how often he is in the store, he maintains a strong knowledge of our stock and promotional items. I have been frequently surprised that I do not have to correct or remind him of anything, even during stressful exam weeks.

I know that Johann is set to graduate with honors and is looking forward to continuing his education at your school. I have helped him in pursuing scholarships and grants and I believe he has earned enough awards to cover his tuition. While he will need to work some to pay for his living expenses, I am confident he can do that and still perform up to your school's strong standards.

I have already spoken to and secured a place for Johann at our sister store in City X. I believe Johann will be an asset to that store, and I know the manager will work with him to accommodate his academic schedule. I believe you will find Johann to be hard-working and completely dedicated to his studies.

I highly recommend you accept Johann's application as I believe he has a very bright future ahead of him. If I can be of any additional assistance in your evaluation of his application, please let me know. I appreciate the time you spent reading this letter and I can be reached at the phone number and email listed above.

Best Regards,

Gerald Jones
Title

Academic Letter of Recommendation from a Current or Former Employer (Undergrad Admission)

SAMUEL PATTERSON

555-555-5555 | Street Address, City, State, Zip | samuelpatterson@emailaddress.com

(Date)

Mr. (Ms.) _____
Title
(Company)
(Address 1)
(Address 2)

Dear Mr. (Ms.) _____:

Cleo Johnson asked me to write to you regarding her application for admission to your school. I am pleased to recommend her and I believe you will find her a hard-working, attentive, and ambitious student.

Cleo has worked for me the summer between her junior and senior year of high school and returned to work this past holiday season. She has asked to work for me the first month after graduation to save up some for college, but is also very interested in the early admissions program at your university. I believe you should accept her to summer program and will find her to be an excellent student, fully committed to making the transition to college life.

Cleo has demonstrated strong sales, merchandising, and customer service skills during her time working for me. Since she is interested in pursuing a business degree, I think these are excellent competencies to demonstrate. I know that Cleo has earned several scholarships and saved up enough so that she does not have to work her first year and can commit fully to her academic pursuits. She has an opening with me if she wishes to work during the holiday or summer breaks.

To date, I have adjusted Cleo's hours around her school schedule and athletic pursuits, and as far as I know, her work has never come into conflict with these efforts. Cleo has told me that due to dual enrollment and advanced placement, she has several college hours already completed. I know that she has a strong interest in not just completing her bachelor's, but also her master's degree at your school. I think she is well equipped to accomplish that goal.

From everything I know about Cleo, I believe she will prove a solid investment if you admit her to your school. Her drive to succeed will lead her to pursue a degree with a strong passion and represent your school well as a future alum. If I can answer any additional questions regarding Cleo, please contact me at 555-555-5555 or samuelpatterson@emailaddress.com.

Sincerely,

Samuel Patterson
Title

Academic Letter of Recommendation from a Current or Former Employer (MBA)

MARY JANE JONES

555-555-5555 | Street Address, City, State, Zip | maryjanejones@emailaddress.com

(Date)

Mr. (Ms.) _____
Title
(Company)
(Address 1)
(Address 2)

Dear Mr. (Ms.) _____:

I am writing to you on behalf of Pamela Adams to recommend her for your MBA program. Pamela has worked for me at XYZ Consulting Corp. for five years. I hired her out of college as a Marketing Specialist and promoted her to Team Leader two years later.

Pamela recently expressed her interest in pursuing an MBA so she can progress into roles of executive management. We have planned a schedule for her to pursue her MBA in your program while continuing in a consulting role with my company. I believe Pamela is more than capable of excelling in both pursuits, but I am completely committed to adjusting her load as needed to facilitate her academics.

Over the last five years, I have found Pamela to be innovative and highly-focused on customer needs. Please consider the following highlights:

- Demonstrates a keen ability to evaluate client requirements and transform them into effective marketing campaigns with high return-on-investment.

- Identifies opportunities to leverage social media and digital campaigns to off-set the expense of traditional marketing efforts.

- Creates content for client websites and makes adjustments as needed to optimize SEO efforts.

- Manages budgets and resources effectively and consistently delivers assignments on-time and on-budget.

I believe Pamela will prove to be a dedicated student who can offer her classmates insight on aspects related to marketing and customer relations. I highly encourage you to admit her to your MBA program and if I can provide you any additional information, please let me know. You can reach me at 555-555-5555 or at maryjanejones@emailaddress.com.

Sincerely,

Mary Jane Jones
Title

Academic Letter of Recommendation from a Current or Former Employer (Law School)

KATIE O'MALLEY

555-555-5555 | Street Address, City, State, Zip | katieomalley@emailaddress.com

(Date)

Mr. (Ms.) _____
Title
(Company)
(Address 1)
(Address 2)

Dear Mr. (Ms.) _____:

I am pleased to write to you today to recommend Eric Smith for your law school program. Eric has been working for my publishing company for two years while completing his bachelor's degree at State University. I find him to be well-organized, reliable, and an effective problem-solver.

When I hired Eric, he told me he was interested in pursuing a law degree and most recently he has set his sights on your program. Over the last few months, he has rigorously studied for and performed admirably on the LSAT. He has also been volunteering to work with our legal team and learned a great deal about intellectual property and contract law.

Eric handles confidential communications with discretion while making sure other aspects of my office run smoothly, including scheduling, billing, and payroll. Managing these aspects of my office requires knowledge of several software applications and Elliot picked them up really quickly. He has also done a great job of maintaining my company website.

Eric shows dedication to his work both in my office and his academic pursuits. He will graduate with honors this spring, and his ability to maintain a high GPA while working demonstrates his talent for balancing his schedule, prioritizing work, and delivering on his commitments. I believe these are skills that will serve him very well in law school.

In conclusion, I highly endorse Eric's application to your law program. If I can be of any additional assistance as you consider him for admissions, please let me know. You can reach me at the contact information listed above. Thank you for your time.

Sincerely,

Katie O'Malley
Title

Academic Letter of Recommendation from a Current or Former Employer (Graduate School)

DR. SHELDON SMITH

555-555-5555 | Street Address, City, State, Zip | sheldonsmith@emailaddress.com

(Date)

Mr. (Ms.) _____
Title
(Company)
(Address 1)
(Address 2)

Dear Mr. (Ms.) _____:

I am writing to you on behalf of Amber Smith, recommending her for admissions to your graduate program for nurse practitioners. Amber was an excellent addition to our nursing staff and St. John's Hospital while she was completing her RN degree. Upon gaining her license, she elected to stay with us and has worked effectively in our emergency room, operating room, and maternity ward over the last several years.

While Amber has proven to be highly competent in a hospital advisor and an exceptional caregiver, I know she has a strong interest in pursuing a higher degree and transitioning to an office setting. After watching Amber work with patients with a wide-range of medical needs, I am confident she will excel in working with a regular patient group.

Amber has excelled in all of her work, from the high-stress setting of emergency and operating rooms to mundane patient paperwork. She performs all of her duties without complaint, even at the end of a long shift. She is bright, positive, and committed to spending her life caring for patients.

Additionally, I believe Amber has the skills to excel in school because I watched her maintain a high GPA while she was completing her RN degree when we first hired her. Even then, she excelled in balancing school, work, and her personal life. I believe she will make an exceptional nurse practitioner and encourage you to admit her to your program.

If you need any additional information regarding Amber, I will be happy to speak with you anytime. Thank you for reading this letter; if you need to reach me, please feel free to contact me at the phone number or email listed above.

Sincerely,

Dr. Sheldon Smith

Academic Letter of Recommendation from a Current or Former Employer (Scholarship)

JESSICA JONES

555-555-5555 | Street Address, City, State, Zip | jessicajones123@emailaddress.com

(Date)

Mr. (Ms.) _____
Title
(Company)
(Address 1)
(Address 2)

Dear Mr. (Ms.) _____:

I am writing to you on behalf of Sarah Miller to recommend her for your scholarship to State University. Sarah has worked as a sales associate at the MegaBookStore I manage while pursuing her associate degree at our local community college for two years now. She is fully committed to her academic pursuits, but still gives her work at my store her full effort.

In the two years she has been working for me, Sarah has demonstrated a strong ability to master product knowledge quickly and provide exceptional customer service. Even when she has worked a light schedule because of exams, she is able to provide our customers with information about product availability and order status.

I know that Sarah will graduate with honors this spring and has been accepted to the degree program of her choice at State University. She also intends to continue working part-time while pursuing her studies and I have arranged for her to have a position at our sister store in City X. The manager in that location will accommodate Sarah's school schedule and I am confident she will prove a valuable member of his team.

While Sarah qualifies for financial assistance and has secured some grants to help with her education costs, I know your scholarship would be invaluable to helping her pursue her goals. I know you receive hundreds of applications each year, but I am confident Sarah will distinguish herself and represent the interest of your scholarship fund well.

I highly recommend you back Sarah with your scholarship and would be happy to answer any questions you might have in this regards. I believe she has a very bright future ahead of her and appreciate the time you took to read this letter. Please feel free to call me at 555-555-5555 or email me at jessicajones123@emailaddress if I can be of any further assistance.

Best Regards,

Jessica Jones
Title

Academic Letter of Recommendation from a Current or Former Teacher (Scholarship)

DR. JACQUELYN SMITH

555-555-5555 | Street Address, City, State, Zip | smith_jacquelyn@emailaddress.com

(Date)

Mr. (Ms.) _____
Title
(Company)
(Address 1)
(Address 2)

Dear Mr. (Ms.) _____:

I am writing to you on behalf of Kevin Hall to recommend him for a scholarship to attend State University where he plans to major in Biological Sciences, on a pre-med track. For the last two years, Kevin has been a top student in my intro to biology and human anatomy 101 at Local Community College. From what I have observed of him, his commitment to scientific/academic pursuits is of the highest caliber, and he has a keen scientific mind in development.

Kevin has demonstrated a strong passion for research, excelling beyond all other students in my class in his lab work. I have even been able to rely on him to assist other students in the classroom in understanding and completing their assignments. Because of his interest in medical pursuits, Kevin volunteers at the local hospital to familiarize himself with the daily happenings of a hospital environment.

I believe Kevin is going to be a high performing student, but I know he needs financial assistance to reach his full potential. While he dual enrolled in high school and got some of his necessary credits out of the way early, Kevin has spent two years at our community college because of his need to work part-time to offset his living expenses. He has earned grants and scholarships to cover his tuition at State University, but your scholarship would help ease the burden of everyday expenses and help his excel in his studies.

For all of these reasons, I believe Kevin is an excellence candidate for your scholarship award. If I can be of any additional assistance or answer any more questions about Kevin, please feel free to contact me at the phone number or email listed above.

Sincerely,

Dr. Jacquelyn Smith

Academic Letter of Recommendation from a Current or Former Employer (Scholarship)

KENDRA WILSON

555-555-5555 | Street Address, City, State, Zip | kendrawilson123@emailaddress.com

(Date)

Mr. (Ms.) _____
Title
(Company)
(Address 1)
(Address 2)

Dear Mr. (Ms.) _____:

I am writing to you on behalf of Rebecca Samson to recommend her for your scholarship program. Rebecca has been accepted and plans to attend University of State in the fall and your scholarship award would prove invaluable in helping her achieve her full academic potential.

I have been Rebecca's manager at LargeRetailOutlet for two years while she works part-time, mainly during summers and holiday seasons. Rebecca comes from a large family that supports her academically but is unable to help her financially in her college pursuits. I know she has dedicated a significant amount of her income to savings and has already secured a work-study slot and other financial assistance for school, but I feel your scholarship would benefit her a great deal.

Rebecca is a clean-cut, hard-working professional with strong product knowledge and excellent customer service. She will graduate with honors in a month and has been admitted into the university's summer program which she will start in June.

I believe Rebecca will embody the values and hard work that your scholarship represents and I highly endorse her for your consideration. If I can be of any additional assistance in your evaluation of her application, please let me know. I appreciate the time you spent reading this letter and I can be reached at the phone number and email listed above.

Best Regards,

Kendra Wilson
Title

Academic Letter of Recommendation from a Current or Former Employer (Scholarship)

PAULA HARRIS

555-555-5555 | Street Address, City, State, Zip | paulaharris23@emailaddress.com

(Date)

Mr. (Ms.) _____
Title
(Company)
(Address 1)
(Address 2)

Dear Mr. (Ms.) _____:

I am writing to you on behalf of Jackie Smith who applied for your scholarship to nursing school last month. Jackie has been accepted to the University of State's Nursing School and is set to begin in the fall. She has worked as a CNA under my management at the City Nursing Home for two years while completing her prerequisites and saving money to earn her RN degree.

Jackie attends classes part-time and works with us full-time, but she wants to reverse that balance while earning her bachelor's degree. I know she has saved a great deal to attend school and we have found her a part-time position at City X's Nursing Home; I believe she would benefit greatly from the support your scholarship would provide.

Jackie is fully committed to providing exceptional patient care and I find her to be extremely patient and tender-hearted with even our hardest clients. She remembers all of our patient's birthdays and stays in contact with family members to facilitate visits and communications. Upon graduation, she wants to work in a hospital environment and I believe she will excel in such a setting.

I believe Jackie has a bright future ahead of her and highly recommend her for your funding and support. If I can be of any additional assistance in your evaluation of her application, please let me know. I appreciate the time you spent reading this letter and I can be reached at the phone number and email listed above.

Best Regards,

Paula Harris
Title

Academic Letter of Recommendation from a Current or Former Employer (Scholarship)

JESSICA MILLER

555-555-5555 | Street Address, City, State, Zip | jessicamiller123@emailaddress.com

(Date)

Mr. (Ms.) _____
Title
(Company)
(Address 1)
(Address 2)

Dear Mr. (Ms.) _____:

I am writing to you on behalf of Andrew Jones to recommend him for consideration of your scholarship award. Andrew has been accepted to State University where he plans to major in finance and marketing. For the last two years, Andrew has worked for me as a sales associate at MajorRetailer while earning his Associate Degree in Business at the local community college.

Andrew is a versatile professional who excels in all aspects of his work, from working with customers to processing shipments and stocking our retail floor. He is hard-working and I never feel like he is slacking off despite his efforts to maintain a high GPA. I have easily accommodated his school schedule and provided him time off during exam cycles, but otherwise he has been an adaptable and agreeable employee.

I can secure Andrew a position at a sister location so he can work while he pursues his studies, but I know Andrew would prefer to focus exclusively on school while preparing for an internship next summer. He has put away money in savings and earned financial assistance from the school, but I believe your scholarship would be highly beneficial in Andrew achieving his full potential.

My daughter received your scholarship several years ago, so I am familiar with the requirements and performance you have come to expect out of your recipients. I am confident Andrew can meet and exceed your standards and highly endorse his application. If I can be of any additional assistance in your evaluation of his application, please let me know. I appreciate the time you spent reading this letter and I can be reached at the phone number and email listed above.

Best Regards,

Jessica Miller
Title

Academic Letter of Recommendation from a Current or Former Teacher (Internship)

DR. SAMANTHA JONES

555-555-5555 | Street Address, City, State, Zip | jones_samantha@emailaddress.com

(Date)

Mr. (Ms.) _____
Title
(Company)
(Address 1)
(Address 2)

Dear Mr. (Ms.) _____:

I am writing to you on behalf of Bill Smith to recommend him for your summer internship research program. For the last two semesters, Bill has worked as my teaching assistant for intro to biology and human anatomy 101 at State University. From what I have observed of him as my assistant and what I know of his academic and professional work, I can fully endorse his application to your program.

I first met Bill when he was a student in my entry-level courses and I mentored him in selecting his academic path during his sophomore year. As a TA, he is organized, helpful to the students, and capable of adjusting to challenges that present themselves throughout the semester. I can entrust Bill to proctor exams and lead effective review sessions with dozens of students. He will make an effective instructor himself someday, but his real passion is in research.

In addition to his assistance in the classroom, Bill has also been helpful with lab work and analysis that I and some colleagues are conducting on platelet rich plasma (PRP) therapy for wound care. Bill is quick to take on extra work on this project and has contributed to some of our findings. Prior to assuming the position of my TA, Bill volunteered at the local hospital to familiarize himself with the daily happenings of a hospital environment.

For all of these reasons, I believe Bill will excel as a researcher and your internship program should provide ample proving grounds for his skill sets. Additionally, I believe you will benefit from his work product. If you need any additional information regarding Bill, please feel free to contact me at the phone number or email listed above.

Sincerely,

Dr. Samantha Jones
Title

Academic Letter of Recommendation from a Teacher/Professor (Internship)

DR. BRANDY LEE

555-555-5555 | Street Address, City, State, Zip | brandylee@university.com

(Date)

Mr. (Ms.) _____
Title
(Company)
(Address 1)
(Address 2)

Dear Mr. (Ms.) _____:

It is my pleasure to write to you on behalf of Victoria Smith, recommending her for your summer internship program. Victoria has completed several courses with me as both an undergraduate and graduate student during her time at State University. She is now half-way through her Masters in Political Science and has expressed a strong interest in the statistic research your internship program offers.

I believe you will find Victoria to be a dedicated research student with a strong aptitude for statistically and quantitative analysis. For the last semester, she has worked as a colleague's research assistant where she is processing much of the statistical data we are using for a book we are co-writing. Her contributions have been of the highest quality and we have asked her to help present our findings at an upcoming symposium. Additionally, she is working on her own research in voting behavior that she will present next year as her graduate thesis.

Victoria will benefit greatly from her time in your program, and I believe she will produce quality work for you. I highly endorse her application and would be happy to answer any additional questions you might have in this regards. Please feel free to reach out to me at the phone or email listed above. Thank you for your time and consideration.

Sincerely,

Dr. Brandy Lee
Title

Academic Letter of Recommendation from a Teacher/Professor (Internship) – Email Format (Personal)

To: sjt@email.com
From: michellesmith@email.com
Subject: Letter of Recommendation for Trish Robinson

Dear Shelly,

Hi there! I hope this letters finds you doing well. I am writing to you on behalf of one of my students, Trish Robinson. I would like to recommend her to you for an internship this summer. She has completed my small business management and advanced financial records courses and did extremely well for me. She has expressed an interest in pursuing an auditing and quality assurance track for a large corporation, and I think she would benefit from your summer internship program.

As a student, Trish showed up on-time to all of her classes and produced high quality work. I believe she would perform to the same high standards for you. You will find her to be polite, eager to learn, and a good team mate to her peers.

If I can answer any additional questions you might have about Trish and her work, please let me know. And if you do not have any openings, please pass along any leads you know of that I can communicate to her. She has a bright future ahead of her and I want to help her realize her full potential. Thank you.

Sincerely,

Michelle Smith
michellesmith@email.com
555-555-5555

Academic Letter of Recommendation from a Teacher/Professor (Internship) – Email Format (Personal)

To: mkh@email.com
From: kimberlyjones@email.com
Subject: Summer Interns

Dear Mary,

I am touching base with you today to recommend Jonathan Martin for your summer internship program. I know you only have a few openings, but I believe Jonathan will prove a valuable addition to your team.

Jonathan worked for us while he was earning his associate degrees and last holiday season when he came back to visit with his parents. We have discussed him working this coming summer, but he really wants to complete an industry-related internship program to help advance his academic and career pursuits. While we were discussing what he should do, I remembered you talking about your summer program and recommended Jonathan look into it.

I understand he has completed the application process and has an interview setup for next week. Before you meet with him, allow me to endorse him and provide a summary of the work he did for me:

* Achieved all individual sales and membership goals and contributed to team accomplishments for sales and customer service ratings.
* Placed and processed customer orders, ensuring quick turnaround and delivery of needed items, even during busy holiday schedules.
* Helped new employees learn stock, merchandise, and sales procedures.

If you need any additional information regarding Jonathan, please feel free to contact me at the phone number or email listed below.

Sincerely,

Kimberly Jones
kimberlyjones@email.com
555-555-5555

Academic Letter of Recommendation from a Teacher/Professor (Internship) – Email Format (Personal)

To: earlellis@email.com
From: mannywilliams@email.com
Subject: Paul Smith

Dear Earl,

Hi there! I hope this email finds you doing well. I am writing you on behalf of Paul Smith because I am his program advisor and am looking to place him in an internship this summer. I believe he would be a good fit for your organization and wanted to reach out to you to see if you have any openings.

Paul is about to complete his junior year in our school's journalism program; he is on the editing track. He has already completed the necessary credits to minor in computer design and wants to merge these skills to work for a publishing company. I believe he could prove instrumental to you in copywriting and design this summer while gaining some hands-on experience in the publishing world.

Paul has maintained a high GPA while in all of his classes and is well skilled in the technical skills he would need to work for you, include Adobe Creative Suites applications. If I can provide you additional information, please give me a call. Thank you and I look forward to hearing from you soon.

Sincerely,

Dr. Manny Williams
mannywilliams@email.com
555-555-5555

Academic Letter of Recommendation (MBA Program) – Email Format

To: sjt@email.com
From: michellesmith@email.com
Subject: Brittany Williams

Dear Sharon,

I am writing to you on behalf of Brittany Williams, recommending her for admissions to your school of business for the MBA program. Brittany worked for me at XYZ Corporation while she was earning her undergraduate and has developed into a top-rated business line manager since she joined us full-time.

Brittany is well-respected by her direct reports and though she is younger than all of her colleagues, she is among our top producers. Now she wants to earn her MBA so that she can gain a deeper understanding of business management and begin an executive track with the company. I fully support her in these efforts and would like to share a few highlights from Brittany's work:

* Owns accountability for a 10-member business unit that is responsible for generating $10M income.
* Manages multiple projects well by prioritizing the most important tasks and creatively addressing issues when they arise to ensure projects stay on-track and on-budget.
* Excels in a cross-functional environment and has taken on the task of selecting and mentoring a summer internship program.

Brittany maintained a high GPA while working for me and obtaining her undergraduate degree, and I fully support her effort to complete her MBA now. Therefore, I will accommodate her schedule however I need to so that she can place her studies first. If you need any additional information regarding Brittany, please feel free to contact me at the phone number or email listed below.

Sincerely,

Michelle Smith
michellesmith@email.com
555-555-555

Academic Letter of Recommendation (Graduate School, Accounting) – Email Format

To: jamestsmith@email.com
From: nicolehroberts@email.com
Subject: Letter of Recommendation for Elliot Thomas

Dear James Smith,

Elliot Thomas asked me to write to you, recommending him for admission to your Graduate Program in Accounting and I am pleased to do so. Elliot has been working as a payroll and accounting clerk in my office for two years. I hired him upon earning his Bachelor's in Accounting from State University and have been impressed with his work to date. Please consider:

* He processes payroll data for more than 100 employees and ensures on-time payment of bi-weekly payroll for salaried, full-time, and part-time personnel.
* He completes journal entries for several multimillion-dollar bank accounts quickly and accurately.
* He works on special tax projects and completes tax work for expats at the height of tax season.

Elliot has now expressed an interest in completing a master's degree in accounting and CPA credentials. I believe Elliot will make an excellent corporate accountant for either a public or private enterprise and support him in these endeavors. He has elected to pursue his studies full-time, but I will have a position open for him if he decides to return to us upon graduation.

I strongly endorse Elliot's candidacy for your graduate program and would be happy to answer any additional questions you might have about his work. Please feel free to contact me at the phone number or email listed below if I can be of further assistance. Thank you for your time.

Sincerely,

Nicole H. Roberts
nicolehroberts@email.com
555-555-5555

Academic Letter of Recommendation
(Graduate School, HR) – Email Format

To: harrywilliams@email.com
From: robinlsmith@email.com
Subject: Letter of Recommendation for Fredrick Jones

Dear Harry,

Fredrick Jones has requested that I write to you to recommend him for your graduate program in Human Resources Management. I am happy to offer my highest endorsement of his candidacy. I hired Fredrick after his graduated from University of State with his Bachelor's in Learning and Development and he has proven a valuable training asset.

Fredrick began his time with us by developing and leading new-hire orientations for dozens of employees at a time. After completing several professional development courses on adult-learning methodology, he transitioned into our corporate university. Since then he has created two new classes and led a half dozen others in classroom and on-line webinar settings.

I find Fredrick to be an excellent teacher and trainer, so when he explained that he wanted to pursue a graduate degree and work as a teaching assistant while doing so, I knew he would prove to a be a solid benefit to your program. I plan on employing Fredrick part-time while he pursues his degree, but will adjust his work load as needed to accommodate his studies.

 If I can be of any additional assistance in your consideration of his application, please let me know. I can be reached at the phone and email listed below. Thank you for your time.

Sincerely,

Robin L. Smith
robinlsmith@email.com
555-555-5555

Academic Letter of Recommendation
(Graduate School, Journalism) – Email Format

To: darrenjamessmith@email.com
From: thomasjwilliams@email.com
Subject: Letter of Recommendation for Cheryl Miller

Dear Darren,

I am writing to you to recommend Cheryl Miller for your graduate program in journalism. I have been Cheryl's editor at Metropolitan Newspaper for five years, managing her from working on the copy desk to a beat reporter for our entertainment and business sections.

Cheryl has proven to be a talented interviewer and delivers on assignments with quick turnaround times while covering entertainment events and business news for the area. She has a keen sense for identifying interesting leads and pursuing stories that have received positive feedback from our subscribers and advertisers.

Recently, Cheryl expressed an interest in attending graduate school and possibly transitioning into teaching as she and her husband start a family. As an alumnus of your school, I know that Cheryl will fit in well to the graduate program. She brings a great passion for writing, photography, and layout to her work and I'm sure that will lead to several positive contributions to your programs.

I highly recommend Cheryl and would be happy to answer any questions you might have regarding her work or character. Please feel free to call me or email me at the contract details listed in my signature if I can be of any more assistance.

Sincerely,

Thomas J. Williams
thomasjwilliams@email.com
555-555-5555

Academic Letter of Recommendation
(Graduate School, Music) – Email Format

To: georgeomalley@email.com
From: kimberlysmith@email.com
Subject: Letter of Recommendation for Julie Jones

Dear George,

I am writing to you on behalf of Julie Jones to recommend her for your graduate program in music. Julie is a very talented pianist, guitarist, and vocalist and has done an excellent job at developing educational programs at our community center.

She has worked for us since high school on a part-time/temporary basis and has helped develop some beautiful holiday program for our community members. In addition to her work on special programs and projects, Julie has provided assistance with special events such as weddings and birthdays.

Julie is already an excellent teacher, leading small groups and one-on-one tutoring sessions for students of all ages, but her desire to pursue a master's degree and a higher level in teaching comes as no surprise. I will miss the work Julie does with us, but I strongly endorse her application to your Graduate Program in Music.

If I can answer any additional questions about Julie's work with us or provide you with any recordings of the programs she has lead, please let me know. I can be reached at the phone number and email address listed below. Thank you for your time and consideration in this matter.

Sincerely,

Kimberly Smith
Program Coordinator, Local Community Center
kimberlysmith@email.com
555-555-5555

Academic Letter of Recommendation
(University Admissions) – Email Format

To:sjt@email.com
From: maryannewilliams@email.com
Subject: Letter of Recommendation for Jason Robinson

Dear Sarah,

I am writing to you on behalf of Jason Robinson to recommend him for admission into your university. Jason worked as a sales associate in my jewelry store during this last Christmas season, the summer in between his junior and senior year, and the Christmas season the year before last. He quickly learned my product selection and has proven himself one of my highest grossing sales associates.

Please consider the following highlights:

* Jason is a clean-cut, outspoken, hard-working employee who provides excellent customer service and has formed a group of clientele that request him when shopping for Christmas gifts or special occasions.
* Jason maintains a 3.9 GPA and is working hard to earn scholarships and save for college. He accomplishes this while running track and field and cross-country.
* Jason is fully bilingual in Spanish and English and has expressed an interest in studying abroad after his sophomore year. He is also interested in your work-study program.

I believe Jason will prove a strong student and will excel at your school. If I can be of any additional assistance in your evaluation of Jason's application, please let me know. I appreciate the time you spent reading this letter and I can be reached at the phone number and email listed below.

Best Regards,

Mary Anne Williams
maryannewilliams@email.com
555-555-5555

Academic Letter of Recommendation (Business School) – Email Format

To:suzansmith@email.com
From: paulwilliams@email.com
Subject: Letter of Recommendation for Isaac Robinson

Dear Suzan,

As William Thatcher' manager at XYZ Inc., I have been highly impressed with his professional accomplishments and work ethic for more than five years. It is now my pleasure to recommend him for admissions to your business school.

William came to me several months ago and told me he wanted to complete his MBA so he could advance into management roles in our company, and I am happy to support his efforts in this regards. As you consider him for admission, allow me to point out some of his achievements:

* William produced significant results while working on seasonal marketing campaigns and evangelizing products at trade shows and industry events.
* William proved vital to generating a significant amount of positive news coverage for several product launches, helping ensure successful revenue performance for what became multimillion-dollar product lines.
* William is well liked by our clients because he places such a strong emphasis on quality and delivering on expectations.

Confident you will be pleased to have William as a part of your program, I highly endorse his application. If I can be of any additional assistance in this matter, please feel free to contact me at the number below.

Sincerely,

Paul Williams
paulwilliams@email.com
555-555-5555

Academic Letter of Recommendation
(Graduate Program, Political Science) – Email Format

To: hkw@email.com
From: michaelhjones@email.com
Subject: Letter of Recommendation for Jonathan Matthews

Dear Helen,

It is my pleasure to write to you on behalf of Jonathan Matthews, recommending him for your graduate program in political science. My first impression of Jonathan came as a stand-out student in a large lecture for American Federal Government. I had the opportunity to get to know him better in my presidential politics course his junior year.

Even though Jonathan was majoring in journalism, he excelled in political analysis and research and made insightful contributions to class discussion, indicating that he did more than just the required reading for the course. Additionally, I found his paper submissions to be comprehensive and high quality, particularly his work regarding the differences in political coverage by national and local news sources.

Since Jonathan expressed an interest in political campaigning, I recommended him for an internship with a local candidate. Congressman Smith said Jonathan was a solid team member, writing excellent press reports and working to generate as many positive news pieces as possible during the election cycle. He also said that Jonathan did wonders for his social media presence.

I highly endorse Jonathan for your graduate program and believe he will prove an asset to your university. If I can provide you with any additional information or be of any further assistance in your consideration of Jonathan's candidacy, please feel free to contact me at the phone or email listed below. Thank you for your time and consideration.

Sincerely,

Dr. Michael Jones
michaelhjones@email.com
555-555-5555

Academic Letter of Recommendation
(University Admissions) – Email Format

To: matthewking123@email.com
From: jsmithjones@highschool.com
Subject: Letter of Recommendation for Julian Scott Keith

Dear Matthew,

Julian Scott Keith has been one of my prize students for several years and he has recently asked me to endorse his application for admission to your school. I am pleased to do so and would love to tell you a bit about Julian and his accomplishments.

It has been my privilege to have Julian as a student for biology honors his sophomore year and anatomy his senior year. I have also gotten to know a great deal about Julian as the sponsor of our school's National Honor Association (NHA) of which is he has been a member for three years. Please allow me to highlight some of Julian's strong points from my perspective as his teacher and mentor.

* Displays a strong curiosity in the sciences and laboratory work, earning top marks in all science courses.
* On track to graduate among the top of his class.
* Participates in fundraising and charity events as well as academic contests.
* Tutors local elementary students in math and reading.

I find Julian to be well deserving of an education at a quality university such as yours, and I believe he will prove a solid member of your student body and future alumni association. I appreciate the time you have spent reading this letter. If I can be of any additional assistance, please feel free to call me at or email or call me at the information listed in my signature below.

Best Regards,

Jennifer Smith-Jones
jsmithjones@highschool.com
555-555-5555

Academic Letter of Recommendation
(School of Business) – Email Format

To: dlpierce@email.com
From: mollywright@email.com
Subject: Letter of Recommendation for Janelle Robinson

Dear David Pierce,

I am writing you to recommend Janelle Robinson for admissions to your university's school of business. I have had the pleasure of coaching Janelle in soccer for four years and instructing her in Spanish her freshman and sophomore years of high school.

Please allow me to highlight some of things I have observed about Janelle during this time:

* Displays a strong commitment to athletic and academic pursuits, leading her team as captain to finish third and second in the state the last two years while earning a top five ranking in a 300+ member graduating class.
* Deeply involved in community organizations, volunteering at summer soccer camps to help teach children the basics of soccer skills and teamwork.
* Travelled on church-sponsored mission trips to Spanish-speaking countries where she helped build homes and honed her Spanish skills.

Sarah has expressed a strong interest in pursuing international business studies at university while continuing to strengthen and expand her foreign language abilities. I believe you will find her to be a highly successful member of your student body and recommend you accept her application. If I can provide you with any additional information, please contact me at the phone and email address listed below. Thank you for your time.

Sincerely,

Molly Wright
mollywright@email.com
555-555-5555

Academic Letter of Recommendation
(Graduate School, Accounting) – Email Format (Personal)

To: janicelong@email.com
From: davidlsmith@email.com
Subject: Letter of Recommendation for Isaac Robinson

Dear Janice,

Hi there! I am writing you today on behalf of Melissa Smith to recommend her for admissions to your graduate program in accounting. Since you and I have been friends for years, you know I do not endorse candidates lightly so I hope you will consider that when I say that I believe Melissa will make a fine addition to your program.

I hired Melissa fresh out of college and have been impressed with her work to date. While working for me, she has expanded her accounting knowledge and stepped up to handle several key projects. Please consider the following highlights:

* Processes payroll for more than 100 employees every two weeks, including pay for salary, full-time, commission, and part-time personnel.
* Completes, reconciles, and verifies journal entries for several bank accounts quickly and accurately.
* Enters data in QuickBooks and provides training for new staff members as needed.
* Helps the Comptroller prepare for internal and external audits and tax filings.

Melissa has expressed an interest in advancing with the company, and we both believe earning a Masters in Accounting and CPA credentials will benefit her in this regards. Melissa is going to vacate her position with us to dedicate herself completely to her studies, but I would gladly rehire her upon completion.

I strongly endorse Melissa's candidacy for your graduate program and would be happy to answer any additional questions you might have about her work. Thank you and I look forward to hearing from you soon.

Sincerely,

David L. Smith
davidlsmith@email.com
555-555-5555

Academic Letter of Recommendation (Graduate School, HR) – Email Format (Personal)

To: stevenasmtih@email.com
From: teddyrobinson@email.com
Subject: Recommendation for Patricia Jones

Dear Steven,

Hi there! I wanted to touch base with you today to recommend Patricia Jones for your graduate program in Human Resources Management. I hired Patricia after she graduated from University of State with her Bachelor's Degree in Psychology and Education and she has proven a valuable training asset. Please consider the following highlights:

* Develops and leads new-hire orientations for dozens of employees at a time that leverage adult-learning methodologies and a multi-media approach.
* Creates and leads courses for our corporate university, delivering training in both classroom and on-line webinar settings.
* Communicates changes in corporate procedures and policies to more than 250 employees, ensuring full understanding and compliance companywide.

I find Patricia to be an excellent teacher and trainer, so when she came to me and said she wanted to complete her master's degree to transition in management career path, I fully supported the idea. I highly endorse her candidacy for your program and if I can be of any additional assistance in your consideration of her application, please let me know.

Sincerely,

Teddy Robinson
teddyrobinson@email.com
555-555-55555

Academic Letter of Recommendation (Business School) – Email Format (Personal)

To: walterstevens@email.com
From: davidjones@email.com
Subject: Letter of Recommendation for Eric Smith

Dear Walt,

Hi there! I hope this email finds you doing well. I wanted to touch base with you to recommend Eric Smith for your business program. I understand that Eric has already submitted his application and has an interview scheduled with you next week.

Eric has worked for me for two years while finishing his senior year of high school and then wrapping up his associate's degree at our local community college. I find him to be hard-working, punctual, and good with his teammates and customers. Please allow me to highlight a few of his achievements:

* Key member of a team that produced $10M annual revenue.
* Proved vital to the development and delivery of a proposal that landed a $2M on-going contract expansion with a key strategic client.
* Helped ensure our records were up-to-date and accurate for a major audit review which we passed with no major findings.

I highly recommend Eric for your program and will be happy to answer any questions you might have about his work. Thank you for your time and I hope to hear from you soon.

Sincerely,

Dr. David Jones
davidjones@email.com
555-555-5555

Academic Letter of Recommendation (Graduate History Program) – Email Format (Personal)

To: jamesjones@email.com
From: eljames@email.com
Subject: Letter of Recommendation for Jason Newlin

Dear James,

I am writing to you on behalf of Jason Newlin and recommending him for admission into your graduate school's history program. Jason completed several of my courses, including History of Southern Wars which we originally co-developed at the University of State. I have found him to be an excellent student and passionate about history. Additionally, his papers are well-written and thoroughly researched.

Jason will graduate from our program with honors in May and has expressed a strong desire to study up north where his fiancé has secured a job. He has already applied to your program and I believe he will make a find addition to your student body. I just wanted to add my endorsement as you consider him for admissions and perhaps for a teaching assistant position.

If I can answer any additional questions about Jason's work, please give me a call. I will be in and out this week, but can be reached on my cell phone anytime. Thank you for your consideration in this matter.

Sincerely,

Dr. Elizabeth James
555-555-5555 ext.555
eljames@email.com

Academic Letter of Recommendation (University Admissions) – Email Format (Personal)

To: lindseysmith@email.com
From: janetrobinson@email.com
Subject: Letter of Recommendation for Maria Rodriguez

Dear Lindsey,

Hi there! I just wanted to touch base with you today to recommend Maria Rodriguez for admission into your program. I know you are busy considering many candidates, but you know that I do not endorse people lightly. So please review Maria's application with great attention and allow me to communicate some of her positive attributes and achievements.

* Maria is frequently requested by clients shopping for Christmas gifts or special occasions and has even helped clients during her time off the clock.
* Maria maintains a 3.87 GPA while carrying a college preparatory school schedule and has expressed an interest in being accepted to your early admissions program.
* Maria has a strong work ethic and will be able to maintain her work schedule and academic load while excelling at both.

I highly recommend you accept Maria's application as I believe she has a very bright future ahead of her. If I can be of any additional assistance in your evaluation of her application, please give me a call.

Best Regards,

Janet Robinson
janetrobinson@email.com
555-555-5555

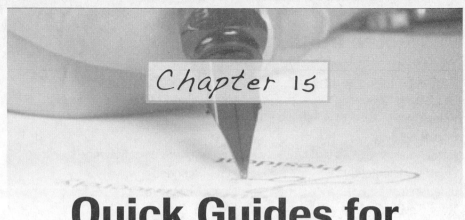

Chapter 15

Quick Guides for Letter Writing

Synonyms List

Ability:	Skill, Competency, Expertise, Capability
Achieved:	Accomplished, Delivered, Completed
Company:	Business, Enterprise, Corporation, Organization, Operation
Changed:	Altered, Modified, Amended, Upgraded
Created:	Designed, Developed, Formulated, Conceived, Innovated, Crafted
Decreased:	Lowered, Reduced, Cut, Slashed
Grew:	Increased, Built, Advanced, Expanded
Earned:	Received, Recognized, Awarded
Fixed:	Corrected, Resolved, Addressed, Problem-Solved, Troubleshot, Turned around
Hired:	Recruited, Engaged, Employed
Increased:	Improved, Elevated, Lifted, Boosted, Enhanced
Managed:	Led, Directed, Headed, Spearheaded, Supervised, Oversaw
Trained:	Instructed, Mentored, Coached, Informed

Character Traits to Focus On

Professional Strengths	**Academic Strengths**
Leadership Skills	Innovation/Creativity
Work Ethic	Analytical Skills
Ethical Behavior	Presentations
Reliable	Intelligent/Subject Mastery
Engaged/Energetic	Well-Rounded
Independent	Time Management
Team Player	Natural Curiosity
Organized	Well Read/Researched
Strategic Planning	Observation
Technical Skills (Be Specific)	
Creative	**Personal Strengths**
Resourceful	Friendly
Client-Focused	Loyal
Good Communications	Dependable
Presentations	Courteous
Negotiations	Mature
Cost Conscience	Patient
	Dedicated
	Strong Integrity

Action Words

Acted	Coordinated	Generated	Programmed
Adapted	Counseled	Guided	Projected
Addressed	Created	Headed	Promoted
Administered	Critiqued	Hired	Provided
Advanced	Customized	Identified	Publicized
Advertised	Cut	Illustrated	Published
Advised	Debugged	Implemented	Purchased
Allocated	Decreased	Improved	Reconciled
Analyzed	Delegated	Increased	Recorded
Appraised	Demonstrated	Informed	Recruited
Approved	Designed	Initiated	Reduced
Appointed	Developed	Innovated	Regulated
Arranged	Diagnosed	Inspected	Remodeled
Articulated	Directed	Installed	Repaired
Assembled	Dispatched	Instituted	Reported
Assigned	Distinguished	Instructed	Researched
Audited	Diversified	Integrated	Restored
Authored	Drafted	Interviewed	Restructured
Automated	Edited	Introduced	Retrieved
Balanced	Educated	Invented	Revitalized
Budgeted	Eliminated	Launched	Saved
Built	Enabled	Led	Screened
Calculated	Encouraged	Managed	Solidified
Catalogued	Enforced	Marketed	Solved
Chaired	Engineered	Mediated	Specified
Coded	Enhanced	Moderated	Spoke
Collaborated	Established	Monitored	Standardized
Collected	Evaluated	Motivated	Stimulated
Communicated	Examined	Negotiated	Streamlined
Compiled	Executed	Operated	Strengthened
Completed	Expanded	Organized	Summarized
Composed	Expedited	Originated	Supervised
Computed	Extracted	Overhauled	Systemized
Conceptualized	Facilitated	Performed	Tested
Conducted	Fashioned	Planned	Trained
Consolidated	Forecasted	Prepared	Trimmed
Contracted	Formulated	Presented	Upgraded
Contributed	Fortified	Prioritized	Wrote
Controlled	Founded	Processed	
Converted	Furthered	Produced	

Conclusion

After sifting through 15 chapters and dozens of sample letters of recommendation, you should have everything you need to write a powerful letter. If you still have doubts about writing a great letter of recommendation, go back and review whatever chapter you're having difficulties with.

While the art of letter writing has gone considerably down, everyone has the ability to write strong business communications. Even the poorest writer can put together five well-worded, grammatically correct paragraphs advocating a candidate for a professional or academic position with the tips and strategies presented in this book.

Just remember, the business letter is not a social networking site or the comments section of an online news article. It is very important to be professional and error-free while writing these letters. With that said, if you follow all of the guidelines outlined in this book, your letter will be well worth reading.

I congratulate you on the future letters you will be writing and the impact you will make on the professional and academic pursuits of your friends and associates. Additionally, I know you will be stocking up loads of positive networking karma by writing great letters. Furthermore, if you need a letter of recommendation from a friend, be sure to hand them this book so you know their letter for you will rock as well!

Contributors

Shannon Bow O'Brien
Professor/Lecturer
University of Texas

Fred Coon
CEO
Stewart, Cooper, & Coon

Steve Elcan
Regional Sales Director
Oracle

Paula Rue
Human Resources Director
Economic Recovery Group, LLC

Valerie El-Jamil
Executive, Career, &
Transitions Coach
Consultant

Bibliography

Allen, Jeffrey G. (1997) *The Complete Q&A Job Interview Book, 2nd Ed.* New York: John Wiley & Sons.

Bodine, Paul (2010) *Perfect Phrases for Letters of Recommendation,* New York: McGraw Hill.

Coon, Fred (2011) Ready, Aim, Hired: Survival Tactics for Job & Career Transition, 3rd Ed. Phoenix: GAFF Publishing.

Hewitt, Janice, "Choose active, precise verbs," www.owlnet.rice.edu (Cain Project)

Sarmiento, Kimberly (2009) *Writing Effective Resume Cover Letters.* Ocala: Atlantic Publishing Group.

Author Biography

K imberly Sarmiento is a certified professional resume writer and has been writing career marketing documents for professionals at all stages of career progression for five years. She works with executives, mid-level professionals, technical staff, and entry-level employees from a diverse range of industries and geographical locations. Prior to entering this line of work, Kimberly was a journalist covering a wide-range of subjects, from sports to features to city government.

In 2009, Kimberly wrote *The Complete Guide to Writing Effective Resume Cover Letters: Step by Step Instructions*. She earned her master's degree in political science and bachelor's degree in journalism from the University of Florida and is a proud Gator for life! She has two beautiful, energetic children who inspire her daily.

Index